Series Editor: Katherine Harrison

Corporeality:
The Body and Society

Issues in the Social Sciences
Titles in the Issues in the Social Sciences series are published annually. The peer-reviewed series presents current academic research into contemporary social issues in an accessible and engaging style that is designed to immerse researchers and students alike in active debates in the Social Sciences.

Corporeality:
The Body and Society

Edited by

Cassandra A. Ogden and
Stephen Wakeman

University of Chester Press
First published 2013
by University of Chester Press
University of Chester
Parkgate Road
Chester CH1 4BJ

Printed and bound in the UK by the
LIS Print Unit
University of Chester
Cover designed by the
LIS Graphics Team
University of Chester

A catalogue record for this book is available from the British
Library

ISBN 978-1-905929-97-9

Dedicated to the memory of

Dr David Charles Ford

Series Editor
2008–10

"From docker to doctor"

CONTENTS

PREFACE

The *Issues in the Social Sciences* series was conceived with the aim of bringing cutting-edge research in the Social Sciences within the purview of both undergraduate students and experienced researchers. Under the general editorships of Anne Boran and David Ford, seven titles were published between 2003 and 2010; an inspiring backlist which provides the strong foundations on which this, the newest title in the series, *Corporeality: The Body and Society*, is based. This new *Issues* volume is the first in the series to reap the benefit of the expertise of members of an Editorial Advisory Board and has been subjected to peer review. While the quality of the *Issues in the Social Sciences* books has always been high, the rigour of the expert reader who reviewed the manuscript has ensured that the present volume is the strongest contribution to the series to date.

Corporeality: The Body and Society extends the *Issues in the Social Sciences* series into the rich arena of the sociology of the body. The volume contains new research from a range of established scholars and emerging voices in the field, covering diverse topics and case studies that reflect the heterogeneity and currency of the subject matter. What unites the chapters is their authors' concern with how the body operates within, and is understood or constituted through, its broader social functions: its consumption and expulsion practices, its capabilities and dis/abilities, its interactions with other bodies and the processes of representation through which we communicate our bodies – alive or dead – to ourselves and others. The research contained in the present volume is complex and challenging, in keeping with the series' emphasis on currency and innovation. The main objective of the series, though, is to present new ideas in an accessible style for the benefit of scholars at all levels. In this respect, *Corporeality: The Body and Society* is a useful addition to the series, presenting complexity of thought in truly approachable terms.

Katherine Harrison
Series Editor
October 2012

ACKNOWLEDGEMENTS

We would like to thank University of Chester Press, in particular Sarah Griffiths, for the help and dedication in bringing this book to publication. Acknowledgement is also due to the members of the newly appointed Editorial Advisory Board who generously agreed to lend their support to the series in order to ensure its continuation and increase its impact. We are grateful to Brian Howman for his role in organising the conference during which some of the following chapters were debuted; to the students and staff of the Department of Social Studies and Counselling at the University of Chester who contributed ideas and suggestions during the planning of the book; and to the contributors whose work makes this volume an invaluable addition to the *Issues in the Social Sciences* series. In addition, the editors would like to thank the following people individually:

Cassandra A. Ogden is indebted to a number of colleagues for their support, advice and wisdom during the creation of this book. I would especially like to acknowledge Peter Cox, Katherine Harrison and Steve Wakeman, who are always available to debate ideas and offer invaluable support. Most of all, I would like to thank the late David Ford who was always keen to give his own sociological perspective on virtually anything that we discussed. His passion for sociology was infectious and this, along with his warm and generous personality, will never be forgotten. Thanks, further, to my family, especially Greg and Elvie Ogden who will remain my inspiration to try to change things for the better.

Stephen Wakeman would, first and foremost, like to thank Katherine Harrison for giving him the chance to work on this project, and Cassandra Ogden for sharing the load – they have both been a pleasure to work with. I would also like to thank everyone in the Department of Social Studies and Counselling at the University of Chester for their help, support and guidance during my time there as a student and, more recently, as a team member. Likewise, I am grateful to Toby Seddon, Judith Aldridge, Jo Deakin and David Gadd of the Centre for Criminology and Criminal Justice at the University of Manchester for their continued guidance in my academic endeavours. And finally, I am grateful to Lisa Wakeman for making everything matter.

CONTRIBUTORS

Michael S. Drake is Lecturer in Sociology at the University of Hull. His research and writing is interdisciplinary, applying social and political theory to the study of organised violence, the body, culture, identity and representation, and historical sociology. He is author of *Political Sociology for a Globalizing World* (Polity, 2010), which sets out new approaches to the study of the political dimensions of social life, focusing on the disjunction between ossified political institutions and the fluidity of contemporary social expectations and new forms of political action. He has also published a critical analysis of the comparative political significance of the different public receptions of the war dead from Iraq and Afghanistan in the UK and the USA, articles on violence and war in the emerging global (dis)order of the twenty-first century, and on cultural representations of collective identity. Ongoing work includes studies of popular contemporary literature as poetic sociology (on which he is editing a book with international colleagues in the Aalborg-Cork-Hull research network), and work focusing on the body in culture, politics and society.

Elizabeth Ettorre is a distinguished feminist scholar and sociologist in the area of substance misuse, genetics, reproduction, gender equality and autoethnography and has an established international reputation in these areas. She is Emerita Professor of Sociology, University of Liverpool, Honorary Professor, University of Plymouth and Docent in Sociology, University of Helsinki and Åbo Akademi University. Her specific areas of interest are: the sociology of substance use including both legal and illegal drugs; gender; sociology of the new genetics; new reproductive technologies; depression and mental health; and autoethnography. She is author of numerous books including: *Health, Culture and Society: Conceptual Heritages and Contemporary Applications* (with J. Robinson, C. Kierans and C. Kingsdon, forthcoming); *Gendering Addiction: The Politics of Drug Treatment in a Neurochemical World* (with Nancy Campbell, 2011); *Culture, Bodies and the Sociology of Health* (2010); *Revisioning Women and Drug Use: Gender, Power and the Body* (2007); *Making Lesbians Visible in the Substance Use Field* (2005); *Reproductive Genetics, Gender and the Body* (2002); *Before Birth: Understanding Prenatal Screening* (2001); and *Women and Alcohol: From a Private Pleasure to a Public Problem?* (1997).

Dan Goodley is Professor of Disability Studies and Education at the University of Sheffield. His work contributes to the development of critical disability studies and aims to understand and eradicate disablism. He is also interested in innovative qualitative methodology including the use of performing arts, discourse analysis and ethnography. He has published prolifically in the field and is recent author of *Disability Studies: An Interdisciplinary Introduction* (Sage, 2011), and co-editor of *Disability and Social Theory: New Developments and Directions* (Palgrave Macmillan, 2012).

Paul Higate is Reader in Gender and Security at the School for Sociology, Politics and International Studies at the University of Bristol. He writes on gender, the military, veterans, peacekeepers and, most recently, private security contractors. He is currently Fellow of the ESRC/AHRC Global Uncertainties Programme and has recently returned from fieldwork in Kabul looking at Private Military Security. Publications include: *Military Masculinities: Identity and the State* (Praeger, 2003) and *Insecure Spaces: Peacekeeping, Power and Performance in Haiti, Kosovo and Liberia* (Zed Press, 2009).

Contributors

Cassandra A. Ogden is Senior Lecturer in Sociology at the University of Chester. Her PhD thesis explored the quality of life and experiences of children with Inflammatory Bowel Disease, which fuelled her interest in the social disgust of the leaky realities of the body. Using a critical disability studies perspective, Cassie has written on disability hate crime, ableist discourses on bodily control, childhood illness experiences and the narrative inquiry technique. She is also one of the key organisers of the internationally renowned *Theorising Normalcy and the Mundane* annual conference.

Jayne Raisborough is Principal Lecturer in Applied Social Science at the University of Brighton. Her work explores the contextual and emotional dynamics of selfhood. She has published in the areas of serious leisure, feminist theory, autobiography, ethical consumption, class and popular culture. She co-edited *Risk, Identities and Everyday Life* (with Julie Scott Jones, 2007) and has recently written about Gok Wan, Jade Goody's death (with Hannah Frith and Orly Klein) and class representations in the *Beano* (with Matthew Adams). Her latest book is *Lifestyle Media and the Formation of the Self* (Palgrave, 2011). She is currently exploring obesity and the social construction of humanhood.

Paul Taylor is Lecturer in Criminology and Deputy Head of the Department of Social Studies and Counselling at the University of Chester. His research interests include victimological perspectives within the coronial process, criminological perspectives within professions and services, including mental health and the history of psychiatry. Recent publication endeavours include a research monograph based upon his PhD study on occupational culture in mental health work (Palgrave

Macmillan, forthcoming) and an edited text for the Policy Press entitled *Dictionary of Criminal Justice, Mental Health and Risk.*

Stephen Wakeman is an ESRC-funded PhD candidate in the Centre for Criminology and Criminal Justice at the University of Manchester, and a visiting lecturer in the Department of Social Studies and Counselling at the University of Chester. His primary research interests are located under the broad rubric of the sociology of intoxication. His doctoral research involves an ethnographic study of heroin and crack cocaine users and dealers in North-West England.

INTRODUCTION

CORPOREALITY: THE BODY AND SOCIETY

Cassandra A. Ogden and Stephen Wakeman

Regardless of how a person spends their day, in a classroom, in work or outside employment, whatever our thoughts, beliefs and experiences of life, all living is embodied. We are corporeal and although we can choose to ignore the creaks, aches, physical characteristics and demands of our bodies, we can never live without or beyond them. Our bodies are usually the first thing we attend to when we wake in the morning. We may empty our bladders and/or attend to daily ablutions in the bathroom, eat some food to stop our grumbling stomachs and carefully select clothing and/or make-up to help conform to culturally accepted norms of beauty and propriety. We are of and within our bodies. Our bodies limit us daily in terms of our capabilities and achievements; even with the increasing intelligence and accessibility of new technologies we cannot wholly escape our bodies. Our physical bodies are only ever in one place at one time and, despite online identities being frequently reified, they are usually still imagined in corporeal form. When we engage with avatars we do so through our physical contact with new technologies. The body, therefore, is difficult to escape even in its most nebulous formations, and the currency of bodily theory and examination in sociological arenas is still, urgently, apparent.

The propensity of social scientists to focus on the arena of the body as a site of both theoretical engagement and empirical exploration has proliferated in the last thirty years, since Bryan

1

Turner's seminal text, *The Body and Society* (1984), arguably set the scene. Prior to this, according to Shilling (2003, p. 17), the body was not neglected completely in sociology, but it experienced an "absent presence" in much sociological work. Durkheim, for example, attends to embodiment when discussing rituals in Totemism (such as tattooing or painting), but often uses such observations to reveal the "real" topics of interest, such as collective conscience (Shilling, 2003, p. 180). Foucault's celebrated works also fail to deal with the body in a phenomenological sense, instead utilising it to highlight the many sites of disciplinary power (Turner, 1984).

The more recent proliferation of diverse sociological approaches to studying the body directly has seemingly coincided with the rise of interpretivist sociology (as opposed to legislative sociology). Bauman (1989) describes this cultural turn as necessary in a pluralist, fragmented world where it is more difficult to see traditional structural sociology as useful. The body can now be studied in its own right as a way to help to understand a host of important topics. This volume, *Corporeality: The Body and Society*, demonstrates some of the unique heuristic and conceptual advantages attainable though utilising the body as a site of sociological analysis. At times the body may be "absent present" in the theory, while at others a phenomenological enquiry is embraced. Nevertheless, all of the chapters enhance the ever-increasing "body" of work on corporeality and society and exemplify rigorous engagement with embodiment. Taken as a whole, the book provides new insights by drawing attention to a number of uniquely contemporary complications regarding the body. The presence of bodies "normalised" and anomalous has remained a reality throughout time, but as political, social and cultural contexts change, so too do sociologists' concerns, and their sites of investigation require relocation. Accordingly, this volume provides a timely opportunity for several new loci of embodiment to be explored and explained.

However, it is not just academic interest that has proliferated in recent years, mainstream social awareness of the body has heightened considerably too. One of the many phenomena that can be utilised as evidence of this increase is the recording and reporting of obesity. The ill-conceived notion of the "obesity crisis" has resulted in various UK government initiatives designed to "combat" obesity and exalt the virtues of a healthy lifestyle. Society appears obsessed with the way the body should and should not look, and various institutions (schools, governments, families, news media) seem more than happy to reinforce these ideas. Such processes are in dire need of the kind of meaningful sociological engagement they are subjected to in this text. Similarly, the 2012 London Paralympics has recently allowed the British public to celebrate disabled people's achievements in professional sport. This event (along with the Olympics) has helped to put the body firmly in the space of public debate. Here, we would note how both disabled and overweight bodies can usefully serve to disrupt people's ideas of independence, dependence, interdependency, fallibility and even "decency". They can also highlight the political, historical and social contexts of all experiences, much like analysis of the control, surveillance and care of those deemed "mentally ill" can. The problems of mental health, in turn, can be understood as engendering "problem bodies" in need of care and/or control. We hope that this text will serve as a reminder that this, too, is an embodied debate.

The primary aim of this book then, is to highlight and attend to a range of contemporary, *embodied* concerns in order to re-state the importance of corporeality for current sociological thought and analysis in the twenty-first century.

One tactic through which this aim is achieved throughout this text is to disrupt and challenge ideas of commonly deemed "deviant bodies". To this end, the following chapters investigate obese bodies, substance-using bodies, disabled bodies, killing and dead bodies, and "dangerous" bodies too. For example, in the binary understanding of "innocent or guilty" bodies in the context of war, "military embodiment" is enmeshed in notions of responsibility, power, nationalism, fairness and the location of bodies both alive and dead. Here, understanding war as an "embodied field" helps to demonstrate its fluidity and uncertainty in the contemporary age and to open it up to new ways of thinking and fruitful research paths. Likewise, the familiar notion of the "irresponsible" drug user in both media discourse and government policy can be challenged from a "body-centred" perspective. The "corporeal pleasures" associated with drug use have been customarily absent from such discourses, yet this significant absence remains somewhat under-researched. There are pressing concerns around gender here, too; the female drug user has been, historically and contemporaneously, subjected to controlling regulatory regimes that the male drug user has not – this is nothing if not an *embodied* disparity. Thus, we would hold, more sustained corporeal analysis of such issues is not only merited, but also *vital* to the furthering of social theory's relevance today.

In bringing together this collection of essays, then, we were presented with the rather pressing problem of providing continuity within the volume as a whole, whilst adequately representing the breadth of the field. Achieving such a goal was no easy task. Whilst some of the chapters here share obvious links, beyond the subject of the body, others do not. Therefore, we decided to group six of the chapters into three pairs, thematically, and then to open and close the book with the two chapters that make more stand-alone contributions to the debate. Our three linked topics are illicit drug use, disability, and war – three areas with a rich and diverse history of analysis from across the social sciences. The result of this is a volume that can be read cover-to-cover, by themed section, or have its individual chapters consulted as necessary. We feel that this approach will not only make the text useful to a broader audience, but more accessible to the student reader too.

The book opens with Jayne Raisborough's analysis of "lifestyle media". Her specific focus is upon the seemingly ever-increasing array of weight-loss TV programmes that now feature on our screens nightly. Raisborough's argument is that such broadcasts form the basis of highly condensed "dehumanising cultural representations" that, in turn, serve to propagate stigmatising discourses surrounding people of weight. Such representations, Raisborough argues, not only vastly over-simplify the complexities of obesity, but they also "foster institutional and interpersonal mistreatment of people regarded as fat and overweight". Astutely noting how the "fat body" is frequently represented through its girth alone, with attention rarely, if ever, paid to the head or face, the chapter concludes by presenting the parallels between representations of the body of weight and the "zombie body". Here, Raisborough calls into question the pervasive belief that an unhinged appetite and loss of control over one's body represent a crisis-like threat to civilisation in urgent need of a rapid response.

Chapters 2 and 3 introduce the first of the volume's themed pairs, focusing on the use of illicit drugs and the interface of drug use with the sociological study of the body. Firstly, Elizabeth Ettorre investigates "using" women. Building on her previous work in this area (1992, 2007a, 2007b), Ettorre poses questions around the consequences of the (often forced) migration of social issues into the body. She specifically refers to drug using women and the reproductive body, arguing that wider social institutions and disciplinary regimes determine which bodies should and should not be reproductive. In this exemplar, the "using" woman's body does not fare well, quickly becoming the subject of tighter and more controlling regimes, and the focus of more penetrative and sustained technologies of surveillance. The core of the chapter focuses on what Ettorre terms "reproductive loss"; the ways in which the "using" female body loses – or more precisely, *has taken from it* – the socially prescribed conditions of reproduction through an amalgamation of processes that render it as "polluted" and "unworthy".

Following this analysis, in Chapter 3, Stephen Wakeman presents his arguments surrounding the heuristic advantages of, and thus the need for, what he terms an "embodied sociology of drug use". Building upon developments in cultural criminology and the sociology of risk taking (Ferrell & Sanders, 1995; Ferrell et al., 2008; Lyng, 1990, 2005), Wakeman presents the rationale behind this call as ostensibly simple; being "high" is nothing if not an *embodied experience*. From this epistemic base, the chapter takes as its two key problematics the use of the formerly legal high, mephedrone, and the concept of "corporeal pleasure". It argues that pleasure – for various reasons – is frequently coded out of dominant explanations as to why people use drugs. Yet, Wakeman contends, corporeal pleasure is central to understandings of the changing nature of contemporary drug use. This is exemplified through the narrative accounts of mephedrone users gathered across the period of time in which mephedrone was transformed from being an easily available legal substance, to a Class B illicit drug. The crux of Wakeman's argument is that legality and pleasure intersect in complex ways, which cannot be understood without due consideration of the corporeal pleasures inherent in, and responsive to, this dialectic interplay.

The second coupled theme visited in this text is disability. Here Dan Goodley leads the way with an introduction to the field of critical disability studies – a field he has helped establish and develop himself (Goodley, 2011). Goodley provides a short essay on this emerging theoretical orientation and its utility by repeatedly posing the same urgent question: "why critical disability studies?" Goodley highlights the potential inherent in this framework through its implicit ability to speak about, with, and sometimes against established sociological and psychological accounts of corporeality – of bodies and society. His argument here can be neatly summarised as such: for Goodley and other scholars working from this position, "disability is *the* space from which to think through a host of political, theoretical and practical issues that are relevant to all".

Chapter 5 takes this theoretical position and neatly exemplifies it in action. Here Cassandra A. Ogden presents her analysis of the "leaky body". As she notes, the fact that we – as a species – frequently "leak" is often overlooked or silenced as repugnant or distasteful, when, indeed, such a realisation can serve usefully as a reminder that we are *corporeal* as well as thinking beings. Here the "normalised aestheticism" of the "perfect" body is called into question through Ogden's research on children and their parents living with Inflammatory Bowel Disease. Building on the critical disability studies framework and the pioneering sociology of Norbert Elias (1994), the chapter calls into question the ways in which "leakiness" is constructed in both biomedical and wider social discourses. Ogden's core claim here is that while these processes legitimise some forms of leakiness under certain socially approved circumstances, they concomitantly create and maintain an "abnormal", "leaky other" with damaging consequences for both these children and their families.

The two following chapters constitute the final themed pairing of the volume – that of the body in relation to war. In Chapter 6, Paul Higate's contribution is based on a case study of Paul Slough, a member of the Blackwater personal security detail that was responsible for the Nisour Square massacre in Iraq in which seventeen Iraqi civilians – men, women and children – were killed. Higate employs Collins's (2008) model of "forward panic" to the Nisour Square incident and in so doing, provides an analysis that transcends the simplistic good man/bad man binary that underlies most other accounts of these events. His argument concludes by proposing the concept of "military embodiment" in respect of questions of responsibility, but also in respect of how sociologists might approach such problematics in the future.

Linked from this, Chapter 7 sees Michael S. Drake's analysis of embodied military matters. Specifically, of what he terms "the returns of war" – the repatriated bodies of service men and women killed on duty in Afghanistan and Iraq. In locating his analysis in the works of thinkers such as Rousseau (1968) and Durkheim (1996), Drake calls into focus the symbolic and instrumental functions of commemoration ceremonies that have taken on a new and revitalised meaning in contemporary social orders such as the UK; the returns of war have come to symbolise – *to embody* – the values of said social orders. Interestingly and importantly here, Drake's analysis transcends borders to highlight the growing difficulties with, and symbolic importance of, such activities throughout Europe and beyond. He concludes by offering the fluid and changing manner in which memorialisation takes place as further evidence of the fluidity and rapid social change that is now such a frequently acknowledged feature of the late-modern West.

Introduction

With Chapter 8, Paul Taylor closes the volume. Taylor's contribution focuses upon the complex relationships between the seemingly exclusive notions of risk and rehabilitative care in "governing the body" of the psychiatric patient. Taylor's chapter breathes new life into some established lines of sociological thought in this area (e.g. Cohen, 1985; Foucault, 1967) by highlighting the similarities that have emerged in mental health and criminal justice legislation in recent years, despite the fact that these fields work from diametrically oppositional ideologies, those of therapy and punishment, of care and control. The result of this, Taylor notes, is a distinct paradox whereby psychiatry's "new aggregated identities of the dangerous" inform and influence the shape of criminal justice measures designed to protect the public. As these dangerous bodies are further constructed, the preventative arms of the criminal justice processes extend ever further into the everyday social lives of the "dangerous body".

As we can see then, this is a diverse yet refined collection of contemporary sociological thought and research. Our guiding vision in bringing these chapters together here is twofold: firstly, we hope to highlight and provide a timely re-statement of the body's centrality in late-modern social thought; secondly, we aim to present this edited collection as a platform from which further analysis might be conducted in the future. We have striven here to represent these fields of study in as accessible a manner as possible, but without sacrificing any of their inherent complexities. Ultimately – we hope – this volume will present its readers with as many questions as it does answers. Questions that will – again, we hope – inspire a new generation of sociologists to tackle some of the issues we have approached here, to think critically about corporeality, about the body and society.

References

Bauman, Z. (1989). *Legislators and interpreters: On modernity, post-modernity and intellectuals.* Cambridge, United Kingdom: Polity Press.

Cohen, S. (1985). *Visions of social control.* Cambridge, United Kingdom: Polity Press.

Collins, R. (2008). *Violence: A micro-sociological theory.* Woodstock, United Kingdom: Princeton University Press.

Durkheim, E. (1996). *The elementary forms of religious life.* New York, NY: Simon and Schuster.

Elias, N. (1994). *The civilising process.* Oxford, United Kingdom: Blackwell.

Ettorre, E. (1992). *Women and substance use.* Basingstoke, United Kingdom: Macmillan.

Ettorre, E. (2007a). Women, drugs and popular culture: Is there a need for a feminist embodiment perspective? In P. Manning (ed.), *Drugs and popular culture: Drugs, identity, media and culture in the 21st Century* (pp. 227–38). Cullompton, United Kingdom: Willan.

Ettorre, E. (2007b). *Revisioning women and drug use: Gender, power and the body.* Basingstoke, United Kingdom: Palgrave Macmillan.

Ferrell, J., Hayward, K. & Young, J. (2008). *Cultural criminology.* London, United Kingdom: Sage.

Ferrell, J. & Sanders, C. (eds) (1995). *Cultural criminology.* Boston, MA: Northeastern University Press.

Foucault, M. (1967). *Madness and civilization: A history of insanity in the Age of Reason.* London, United Kingdom: Routledge.

Goodley, D. (2011). *Disability studies: an interdisciplinary introduction.* London, United Kingdom: Sage.

Lyng, S. (1990). Edgework: A social psychological analysis of voluntary risk-taking. *The American Journal of Sociology, 95*(4), 851–86.

Lyng, S. (ed.) (2005). *Edgework: The sociology of risk-taking.* London, United Kingdom: Routledge.

Rousseau, J-J. (1968). *The social contract.* London, United Kingdom: Penguin.

Shilling, C. (2003). *The body and social theory* (2nd edn). London, United Kingdom: Sage.

Turner, B. (1984). *The body and society* (1st edn). London, United Kingdom: Sage.

CHAPTER 1

TRANSFORMING FAT BODIES: LIFESTYLE MEDIA AND CORPOREAL RESPONSIBILITY

Jayne Raisborough

As the obesity epidemic fills the news hours, weight-loss TV programmes fill day-time viewing and the much sought after 8-9 pm slot in UK television. It seems that, as TV news warns us of the problem – the personal and national cost of obesity; weight-loss TV presents us with the solution – a hearty mix of the right attitude, the right diet and the right exercise. A growing chorus of critical voices are raising rigorous challenges to the obesity science informing the news and other factual reporting (for example see, Campos et al., 2006; Gard, 2010; Evans et al., 2010). More specifically for our purposes, scholars charting the cultural prejudices weaving through that science, observe a denigrating visual imagery of fatness and fat bodies accompanying most factual reportage. In short, this work argues that dehumanising cultural representations not only simplify the complexity of obesity, but fuel everyday stigmatisation of people of weight and foster institutional and interpersonal mistreatment of people regarded as fat and overweight (Carr & Friedman, 2005; Morrison Thomson, 2009). However, less attention has been paid to the ways fatness and fat bodies are represented in weight-loss TV shows. While denigrating imagery is clearly evident, this chapter argues that different mediations of fatness are observable in weight-loss shows. By identifying weight-loss TV shows as a part of a wider genre of lifestyle media, itself defined as that concerned with transformation, this paper maps out a redemptive fat

12

body. However, this is not to suggest that more positive "fat" imagery and representation exists, but to argue that the conditions and means of redemption reveal much of the ways that ideal neoliberal personhood is being imagined, visualised and circulated in popular culture.

Lifestyle TV and Makeover Culture

While reality TV is an ever-sprawling genre and increasingly difficult to define and delineate, Lifestyle TV, a sub-genre, has, for the moment, a defining characteristic – it is mainly concerned with the voyage of transformation (Bell & Hollows, 2005; Palmer, 2004). This is best typified in the narrative device and stylist flourish of the "makeover". The makeover was once a discrete, behind-the-scenes event in day-time magazine TV shows. 1970s programming like the BBC's *Pebble Mill at One* would include a makeover in their format: a woman would be plucked from the audience, displayed as the "before", whisked off for expert intervention, to suddenly reappear as a glamorous "after". What is different today, is that the makeover *is now the show itself,* and little escapes it: cars (*Pimp My Ride*); gardens (*Burke's Backyard*); personal finance (*The Bank of Mum & Dad*); homes (*HomeMade*); parenting (*Nanny 911*); appearance (*What Not To Wear*); and even wedding days (*Pimp My Bride*) are all madeover. The expansion of the makeover both in airtime and in its targets, has resulted in an opening out of the narrative space and time between the "before" and "after". Experts no longer practise their magic behind closed doors, but have become celebrities in their own right: life-coaches, designers, stylists, architects, botanists and specialist cleaners are amongst those who flourish in Lifestyle TV. Additionally, audiences are treated to the participants' *experiences* of being "madeover". There are numerous confessions into handheld cameras and on therapy couches, or alternative spaces such as in front of mirrors *(How to Look Good Naked)*; these are combined with interviews with friends and family, CCTV footage, and a barrage of tests that make visible the progress a participant makes through the journey of transformation (you might recall the swabs in *How Clean Is Your House,* the stool analysis used in *You Are What You Eat* and the battery of medical tests and statistics that comprise *Honey, We're Killing the Kids).* What is inescapable is that the journey of transformation doesn't just happen – one is not simply transported from the before to the after – rather the journey involves a great deal of hard labour, expertise, determination and perseverance (Fraser, 2007; Lewis, 2008).

The changes to the makeover briefly discussed above, are indicative of broad social and cultural changes that Meredith Jones (2008) captures in her term "makeover culture". This term speaks to a current political, economic and cultural context whereby transformation and change become central organising principles of citizenship. She states:

> The cultural logics of makeover culture emphasise continual performances of becoming: improving, growing and developing are all more valued than achieving a point of finality. Good citizens of makeover culture effect endless renovations, restorations and maintenance on themselves and their environments, stretching and designing their faces, their bodies, their ages, and their connections with technologies and other bodies. In turn nothing is ever complete or perfected: everything and everyone is always in need of a literal or metaphorical facelift.
>
> (Jones, 2008, p. 189)

What concerns Jones is that selfhood is being redefined in the makeover culture. As we can see from her quote, just being is no longer enough, rather it is an endless process of *becoming*

14

which stands as the principle marker of selfhood. She stresses that becoming is a "mode of being" (2008, p. 55), transformation becomes the means by which we can all claim a culturally intelligible self in contemporary consumer capitalism. There may be room for an upbeat prognosis of this shift to becoming in the makeover culture. Hakim for example, celebrates women's ability to transform so that they may acquire and continue to accrue what she terms "erotic capital" – "a nebulous but crucial combination of beauty, sex appeal, skills of self-presentation and social skills" (2011, p. 1). However, the incredulous response to her book, *Honey Money*, shows that scholars are politically sensitive to the contextual power relations which still bind people's lives, choices and being, and are suspicious of the ways selfhood is being imagined (see Skeggs, 2004). While we might be concerned with the self-sexualisation that Hakim and others celebrate, other scholars are anxious about what they see as a complicit alignment between the ideal selves circulating in the makeover culture and the needs and demands of neoliberal organisation and rationality. The ideal citizen of the makeover culture is clearly premised on the enterprising, calculating, highly individualised self, required by a creeping marketisation of society, life and selfhood (Bauman, 2007; Honneth, 2004). Critical questions need to be asked then, of the shape and direction of transformation and of the function this serves in current social organisation. There are then, two interesting and timely questions to pose; just who is deemed in need of a makeover in the makeover culture, and just what kind of self is imagined as the result of these endless labours of becoming?

What Jones enables is a contextualisation of Lifestyle TV programming within wider socio-economic contexts and a healthy suspicion of the ways selfhood is being shaped. This project also concerns media scholars operating with

Foucauldian-inspired theoretical frameworks; Toby Miller, for example is interested in the ways that neoliberal rationalities "seek to manage subjectivity through culture" (2007, p. 2), beckoning attention directly to Lifestyle TV shows. Furthermore, Laurie Ouellette and James Hay (2008, p. 2) argue that Lifestyle TV "circulates informal 'guidelines for living' that we are all (at times) called upon to learn from and follow". They conclude that TV, as a promoter and shaper of self-actualisation, operates as a "form of citizen training" (2008, p. 15). Jack Bratich (2006, p. 67) concurs, seeing lifestyle media as "instructional devices that encourage self responsibility, self entrepreneurialism, and self improvement as a neoliberal form of governance". It remains for Ouellette (2009) to underscore this point in her direct demand that Lifestyle TV be seen as a specific *technology* of neoliberal governance.

The Weight-Loss TV Show
Recent years have seen the arrival and spread of a number of Lifestyle TV shows explicitly addressing health and medical matters. This programming is of particular interest because of the increasing number of people turning to Lifestyle TV for information about their health and well-being and for practical assistance. For Ouellette and Hay (2008), this in itself is indicative of the erosion of public welfare provision. They argue that in a "post-welfare society", Lifestyle TV becomes one way in which the once social services can be accessed:

> It is the sign of the times that hundreds of thousands of individuals now apply directly to reality TV programs not only for medical needs, but also for decent housing (*Extreme Makeover: Home Edition, Town Haul, Mobile Home Disasters*), tuition and income assistance (*The Scholar, Three Wishes*), transportation (*Pimp My Ride*), disaster relief (*Three Wishes:*

Home Edition), food, clothing, and other basic material needs (*Random One, Renovate My Family*).

(Ouellette and Hay, 2008, pp. 32–3)

Journalist Steve Mirsky wasn't being sarcastic when he commented that the 43 million Americans without health insurance would be well advised to "sell their conditions to television programs, who would pay for treatment" (2004, p. 19). If the post-welfare society produces a demand for such programming, there is also a concern with the ways health and medical matters are represented and mediatised in a makeover format. Joffe and Staerklé (2007) warn that we should not underestimate the reach and influence of the mass-media in constructing common sense perceptions of illness, sick Others and of a healthy self. Specifically, they caution that themes of health and illness "tend to be constructed in terms of responsibility and blame and associated with social groups . . . They raise questions concerning who is dangerous and threatening, and who should be avoided" (Joffe and Staerklé, 2007, pp. 402–3). Cultural representations of health and illness then, *matter.* The stakes may be raised in terms of obesity, as factual reportage already labours to forge an equivalence between fatness and "badness and sickness" to such an extent that Lee Monaghan (2007, p. 605) suggests that "fat may as well be a four letter word".

There are a number of weight-loss shows, each vying for audience share (and advertising revenue). The most lucrative of these is *The Biggest Loser,* where overweight people compete to lose the most weight each week. Other shows, such as Gillian McKeith's *3 Fat Brides, 1 Thin Dress,* sees overweight brides racing to lose weight to win the (skinny) designer dress of their dreams. There are a raft of shows that set impressive challenges for groups of overweight people to achieve, for example *Fat March,* where a 500 mile trek is to completed, with restricted food intake along the way. What most of these shows share is not just a competitive format – a competition adds urgency, provides a time frame for the loss and the audience's engagement and allows for melodrama – they also share, and circulate, the logics of BMI calculations (Body Mass Index). The BMI reduces obesity to a single measurement drawn from the relationship of height and weight. It is problematic because by isolating weight and height, weight becomes the only variable that can be changed. Weight then, is presented as changeable and it's a small step to then regard weight as *controllable*. Once this step has been made, it is possible to imagine that the health risks argued to accompany weight are *preventable*. The problem of fat thus becomes imagined as being within the personal capacities of an individual to manage. What we see across a range of weight-loss shows are demonstrations that with the right expert help and an (fat) individual's "willpower" – fatness, as a personal and social problem, can be avoided.

Zombie Bodies
Surprisingly, what is unique about weight-loss TV shows is the different representational opportunities afforded to people of weight. Criticisms of factual reportage of obesity have challenged the ways that fatness is represented through the girth of the stomach or the buttocks. News stories of obesity statistics are accompanied by disembodied tums and butts in public places, many spilling from strained clothing or looking clumsy as they lumber in spaces designed to make them appear out of place and comical. Deborah Morrison Thomson's (2009) analysis of television reports argues that fat bodies are rarely filmed in ways that allow heads or faces to be seen. She calls this an act of "spectacular decapitation", which may be an attempt to protect the privacy of people filmed in public places,

but is more likely an act of symbolic violence that removes personhood and individuality along with the head. In a similar vein, Fife (2009) adds that decapitations remove the mouth: a symbolic act that denies the fat body a voice, leaving it to be spoken about and regarded by others. For Murray (2008), the decapitation presents the fat body in ways that invite a culturally specific lipoliteracy. Lipoliteracy refers to shifting sets of cultural meanings that attach to fat bodies. Given that the fat body is presented mainly in terms of risk (to itself and to others, because of its economic cost), lipoliteracy circulates and reproduces everyday knowledge about what the fat body *is,* how it was *caused,* and can immediately index those risks: it also provides an authoritative and informed justification for any discrimination that may follow from such a reading. The act of decapitation is then an act of dehumanisation, a recasting of bodies on to a specific frame of reference and moralising judgement. What is striking about the ways fat bodies are visually depicted is their lifelessness and lack of purpose – and it is this that allows links to be drawn between the fat body and another figure currently at large in the popular imagination – the zombie.

The zombie has long lumbered through popular culture – the undead or living dead are primarily defined by their lack of rational thought. This lack was once the product of a lobotomy enacted by an evil master on the dead, but George Romero's zombie apocalypse horror franchise, presented us with the "new" zombie who was driven only by an insatiable cannibalistic *appetite* (Gunn & Treat, 2005). There are many parallels then, between the fat body and zombie – an appetite unhinged from rationality and self control; a self "taken-over" so that no face or voice is needed; and also a sense of monstrous threat that swelling numbers of zombies/the obese pose to civilisation. However, what makes the zombie such a timely villain is that it represents the antithesis of the makeover culture.

For Jones (2008), betterment and self-improvement are endless. Indeed, she makes the critical point that the activities of becoming are increasingly coded as the activities of life itself. To stop, even if one should believe themselves to be perfected, relegates the self *outside* intelligible life and the self occupies what Jones likens to a "still life" and spaces of the "living dead" (2008, p. 147). Similarly, it is the movement of the makeover culture that echoes Bauman's (2007) insistence that selfhood in advanced consumer societies is predicated not just on "acquiring and possessing" goods and services, rather upon *"being on the move"* (original emphasis, p. 98). The consumer who is *satisfied* constitutes a threat. He concludes that "individuals who settle for a finite assembly of needs ... never look for new needs ... are *flawed consumers* – that is, the variety of social outcast specific to the society of consumers" (2007, p. 99). What the zombie and fat body share is an undiscerning appetite/consumption; glistening piles of junk food which have become so familiar on our TV screens, suggest that fat bodies *eat anything.* What Bauman's outcasts and Meredith Jones's (2008) "living dead" share is a stillness: they have stopped the culturally defined activities that currently define a life worth living and a person worthy of such a life. The fat body and zombie is thus targeted with fears of laziness, greed, inefficiency, and, tellingly of our time, dependency and immobility – all fears of a situated self. Drawing on psychodynamics, Joffe (2007) notes how the projection of the self's anxieties and fears on to the Other serve to condemn the self to a constant vigilance against the return of those projections – often understood in terms of contamination – and to an enduring apprehension, unease and even fear of the Other. So, while the "normal" body cannot "catch" fat (or "zombiness"), it may be nonetheless fearful of the contagious "diseases of will" that those bodies seemingly embody.

Supersize vs Superskinny
However, I stated above that weight-loss shows offer a different representational space for fatness, but this is not to suggest that the zombie fat body is absent. Rather, the zombie fat body plays an important narrative function in the necessary movement of the makeover. I want to discuss this by drawing on a specific show – C4's *Supersize vs Superskinny*. This was first aired in 2008 and now is preparing for its fifth series. As the title suggests, the show is based on a series of comparisons between an overly thin person (coded anorexic) and an overly-weighty person (coded clinically obese). Combining one-to-one consultations/confessions with celebrity doctor, Dr Christian Jessen, the Supersize and Superskinny are firstly confronted with their food choice and eating habits (their weekly food intake is gushed down a plastic tube), before swapping diets for three days. There is a mildly competitive angle, in as much as the "Skinny" and "Sized" are expected to compete to gain/lose the most weight. *Supersize* also shares other characteristics of weight-loss shows; participants are first and foremost *food disordered*; problems with weight are seamlessly translated into the cause of problems in all other spheres of life (Sender & Sullivan, 2008). There is also the now familiar unstinting visualisation of food disordered bodies; lingering camera shots on too sharp collar bones, or dimpled flesh spilling out from drab underwear. Further, *Supersize* reiterates the message that dealing with weight issues is an expression of personal empowerment (Guthman, 2009).

In common with other shows *Supersize* starts with statistical "facts" of weight disorder. And it is here that the zombie body makes it first appearance. As health warnings scroll over a backdrop of tums and butts, the zombie speaks to an undifferentiated mass that this week's participants have the chance to escape. In this regard the zombie body represents a present threat (the participant could belong to that mass) and a future threat (the participant could be returned here if they don't exercise conformity to expert guidance). The zombie body is thus a "before" body, mediated through health and economic risks and threats to a viable and intelligible selfhood. It is clear that these bodies are the ones to cast off: the participant takes a step away from any possibility of a shared fate with each weight reduction. However, *Supersize* also deploy zombie bodies further into their narrative. Once the participant has started the journey of transformation, the zombie body is called upon to add urgency and certainty to the labours faced. *Supersize*, conjures the testimonies of six severely obese people who *embody* a warning to the show's participants. This is one of the few cases where the zombie body actually speaks. Filmed naked on a bed, its immobility underscored by footage of teams of people turning an impossibly distorted body to clean its hidden crevices, the body is denied dignity or privacy but nonetheless it is given a head and a voice from which it issues pitiful laments and warnings – it's too late for me, don't be like me, make the change, take responsibility. As such, the zombie who *is* afforded a voice does so to articulate the ideals of self-responsibility, other zombies are left voiceless. That one of the people died during filming of *Supersize* adds to the urgency of their message and the presumed sad waste of their (unchanged) lives. The zombie body is thus presented in the narrative of "before" and "during" as an abject body to be cast off and escaped from (Morrison Thomson, 2009). As a body and state to be refuted, the zombie is used in Lifestyle TV to incite "manic desires for changing the self" (Ringrose & Walkerdine, 2008, p. 235). As a "before" body it is presented as imprisoning and "taking-over" a normal life, reducing it to a life lived on the margins. As a warning, the zombie body is one denied not only dignity, but motivation or agency – *it just is.*

Yet, the makeover culture proceeds on movement and progression. The endless labours of improvement and the movement through "newly improved" selves requires various opportunities for redemption and rehabilitation (the melodramatic visualisation of which *is* the makeover show). In order for individuals to be cast as makers of their own destiny there has to be intelligible moments of awakenings and rehabilitation built into the tale of transformation – if not, failure would once and for all write us off the registers of personhood. Instead, failure, personal weaknesses and lack are actively sought by stories of transformation. These are the confessions, the realisations of past errors and of faulty relationships with food and increasingly likely in our therapy culture, with our inner selves, that make up the beginning segments of all makeover shows. To confess signals a reflexive maturity and a rational ability to learn from the past and *move on.* Thus the currency of makeover culture depends on the belief that there is the potential and opportunity to start again. And it's here that a wider symbolic representation of fatness and fat bodies is possible.

The participants on *Supersize* have their desire for change immediately rewarded by the acknowledgement of an individuality, a biography and context. We know something about a Sized person "trapped" in the fat body. We know their motivations and struggles and can feel involved when they "dig deep" and we, the audience, can follow their "ups and downs" throughout the show. Their efforts to become better afford them a stronger stake on personhood – even if they fail – for then they can testify to self-development, lessons learnt and a renewed commitment. What we see is a determined but nonetheless cheerful engagement with the process of change. However, it would be a mistake to see this body as the "after" body, for the final weigh-in is only the *start* of the journey of transformation. As the experts of *Supersize* help create a better body, they aim to *replace* the participant back into the makeover culture and back into the endless stream of transformation Jones (2008) envisages. Indeed, that is the "reveal" of the show – a successful handing back of a life to the market.

That said, the fat body is not allowed an easy escape from its zombie fate. The contrasts between the Sized and the Skinny afforded by the show indicate the precarious hold the fat body has upon redemption. Julie and Jade, the respective "size" and "skinny" of one episode, are filmed before their arrival at the food clinic. Jade is filmed preparing a meal for her son in their own home. She is deeply concerned that her own eating problem will affect her son. Her main motivation is to tackle her eating disorder so that she has the energy to be a better parent. Julie, however, is unemployed and lives with her parents. She is filmed whilst being served mountainous plate loads of food by her mother (filmed pouring in a quart of cream into Julie's food). Julie talks enthusiastically about her mum's shepherd's pie while her mum beams with a nervous pride, "I like food because I like eating. I'll eat anything I can get my hands on basically", she says. That Julie has already been presented to the audience as twenty-four stone serves to orchestrate an unfavourable reaction towards her. She is presented as greedy and child-like – a melodramatic contrast to the guilt-ridden Jade. However, if the show is to progress the makeover, Julie has to disavow the abject zombie body and her "still life". Her declared love of food prohibits this, so the show shifts to recast as her as a victim of emotional distress by asking "Have you always been overweight? What happened?"

24

Celebrity Doctor Christian Jessen attempts to contrive a confession or clues for diagnosis:

> *Dr Christian*: Do you think bullying caused you to eat more?

> *Julie*: I don't think so. I wouldn't say I comfort eat as such. I eat because I like food.

> *Dr Christian*: There's two things, there is what we call emotional hunger and physical hunger, and I bet you haven't felt physical hunger for a long time and I think, although you say you don't comfort eat, that there's a large amount of emotional eating in you?

> *Julie*: Yes

It's not clear here whether Julie is acquiescing or agreeing, and there's a degree of confusion in the show's wider narrative of whether Julie was bullied because of her weight, or gained weight through bullying – however, as Room (2003) argues, the key here is not the "truth" but the production of a truth. The show's narrative momentum "leaves few participants able to defend their bodies as not in need of transformation" (Skeggs, 2009, p. 635), or indeed, as able to talk *against* the registers which position them as worthy of expert intervention. What *is* clear is that Julie's success at the reveal is not the loss of weight (she loses very little) but the fact that she has left home, lives independently and was due to start gainful employment. There is a curious mix of responsibility with corporeality here, suggesting that fatness represents concerns less to do with health and economic threats and more to do with concerns about independence, mobility and self-management – all cardinal markers of neoliberal personhood: yet Julie can only hang on to this by *doing* more, by *losing* more – her labours have just begun.

Conclusions

As Meredith Jones has argued, successful selfhood lies not in "being" but rather in "becoming". She says, "in the makeover culture the process of *becoming something better* is more important than achieving a static point of completion" – good citizens are always on the move, engaged in "never-ending renovations of themselves" (2008, p. 1). The "after" in the makeover show may be only the start of further labours, but is a momentary point of compression, when we might see who and what counts as a self. Weight-loss shows are not necessarily "just" about the reduction of the fat body, as they are about a visual rejection of what that fat body currently represents in a limited and denigrating symbolic repertoire. The abject body is that which stands still, and the threat of stillness fuels a contempt and fear for bodies that are purportedly slow, undiscerning, flawed consumers. Butler has recently argued that "a life has to be intelligible *as a life*, has to conform to certain conceptions of what life is, in order to become recognisable" (2009, p. 7). What this chapter suggests is that the registers of recognition cannot be considered apart from wider social and economic organisation and that, in that regard, the pedagogic functions of Lifestyle TV demand further scrutiny for what they may indicate about the construction of a specifically situated selfhood.

References

Bauman, Z. (2007). *Consuming life.* Cambridge, United Kingdom: Polity Press.

Bell, D. & Hollows, J. (eds) (2005). *Ordinary lifestyles: Popular media, consumption and taste.* Milton Keynes, United Kingdom: Open University Press.

Bratich, J. (2006). Nothing is left alone for too long: Reality programming and control society subjects. *Journal of Communication Inquiry, 30*(1), 65–83.

Butler, J. (2009). *Frames of war: When life is grievable?* London, United Kingdom: Verso.

Campos, P., Saguy, A., Ernsberger, P., Oliver, E. & Gaesser, G. (2006). The epidemiology of overweight and obesity: Public health crisis or moral panic? *International Journal of Epidemiology, 35*(1), 55–60.

Carr, D. & Friedman, M. (2005). Is obesity stigmatizing? Body weight, perceived discrimination and psychological well-being in the United States. *Journal of Health and Social Behaviour, 46*(3), 244–59.

Evans, B., Monoghan, L. & Aphramar, L. (2010). *Debating obesity: Critical perspectives.* Basingstoke, United Kingdom: Palgrave.

Fife, K. (2009). Exceeding roles: Negotiating the fat subject in contemporary society, Unpublished paper presented at Cosmetic cultures: Beauty, globalization, politics, practices. 24–26 June. University of Leeds, UK.

Fraser, K. (2007). "Now I am ready to tell how bodies are changed into different bodies..." Ovid: *The Metamorphoses.* In D. Heller (ed.), *Makeover television: Realities remodelled* (pp. 177–92). London, United Kingdom: I. B. Tauris.

Gard, G. (2010). *The end of the obesity epidemic.* London, United Kingdom: Routledge.

Gunn, J. & Treat, S. (2005). Zombie trouble: A propaedeutic on ideological subjectification and the unconscious. *Quarterly Journal of Speech, 91*(2), 144–74.

Guthman, J. (2009). Teaching the politics of obesity: Insights into neoliberal embodiment and contemporary biopolitics. *Antipode, 41*(5), 1110–33.

Hakim, C. (2011). *Honey money: The power of erotic capital.* London, United Kingdom: Allen Lane.

Honneth, A. (2004). Organized self-realization. *European Journal of Social Theory, 7*(4), 463–78.

Joffe, H. (2007). Identity, self-control and risk. In G. Moloney & I. Walker (eds), *Social representations and identity* (pp. 197–213). Basingstoke, United Kingdom: Palgrave Macmillan.

Joffe, H. & Staerklé, C. (2007). The centrality of the self-control ethos in Western aspersions regarding outgroups: A social representational approach to stereotype content. *Culture & Psychology, 13*(4), 395–418.

Jones, M. (2008). *Skintight: An anatomy of cosmetic surgery.* Oxford, United Kingdom: Berg.

Lewis, T. (2008). Transforming citizens? Green politics and ethical consumption on lifestyle television. *Continuum: Journal of Media and Cultural Studies, 22*(2), 227–40.

Miller, T. (2007). *Cultural citizenship: Cosmopolitanism, consumerism and television in a neoliberal age.* Philadelphia, PA: Temple University Press.

Mirsky, S. (2004). A modest proposal for small screening in medicine. *Scientific American, 290*(5), 119.

Monaghan, L. (2007). Body Mass Index, masculinities and moral worth: Men's critical understanding of "appropriate" weight-for-height. *Sociology of Health and Illness, 29*(4), 584–609.

Morrison Thomson, D. (2009). Big food and the body politics of personal responsibility. *Southern Communication Journal, 74*(1), 2–17.

Murray, S. (2008). *The fat female body.* Basingstoke, United Kingdom: Palgrave Macmillan.

Ouellette, L. (2009). Take responsibility for yourself: Judge Judy and the neoliberal citizen. In S. Murray & L. Ouellette (eds), *Reality TV: Remaking television culture* (2nd edn) (pp.

223–42). London, United Kingdom: New York University Press.

Ouellette, L. & Hay, J. (2008). *Better living through reality TV.* Oxford, United Kingdom: Blackwell.

Palmer, G. (2004). "The New You": Class and transformation in lifestyle television. In S. Holmes & D. Jermyn (eds), *Understanding reality television* (pp. 173–90). London, United Kingdom: Routledge.

Ringrose, J. & Walkerdine, V. (2008) Regulating the abject: The TV makeover as site of neo-liberal reinvention towards bourgeois femininity. *Feminist Media Studies, 8*(3), 227–46

Room, R. (2003). The cultural framing of addiction. *Janus Head, 6*(2), 221–34.

Sender, K. & Sullivan, M. (2008). Epidemics of will, failures of self-esteem: Responding to fat bodies in *The Biggest Loser* and *What Not To Wear. Continuum Journal of Media and Cultural Studies, 22*(4), 573–84.

Skeggs, B. (2004). *Class, self, culture.* London, United Kingdom: Routledge.

Skeggs, B. (2009). The moral economy of person production: The class relations of self-performance on "reality" television. *Sociological Review, 57*(4), 627–64.

CHAPTER TWO

USING WOMEN: EMBODIED DEVIANCE, POLLUTION AND REPRODUCTIVE REGIMES

Elizabeth Ettorre

Over the past decades, indeed centuries, scientific and biomedical discourses on the body have become rooted in contemporary culture. As social scientists begin to position bodies centrally in their approaches to society and culture (Martin, 1992; Turner, 1996; Shilling, 2005 and Bordo, 1993), natural scientists and biomedical experts continue to persist with creating techniques to alter the boundaries of these bodies and attempt to close up the spaces between them. Often at times, this has meant that social issues are not only allowed but also forced to emigrate to our bodies. The, at times, troubling social and cultural issue of drug use, emigrates in this way. In effect, we have all become unwittingly members of a captive audience to the cultural spectacle of drug use. Of course for drug using women this spectacle has damaging consequences.

In this chapter, I turn our attention to a type of embodiment that is on offer to drug-using women, the reproducing body. I want to draw attention to the regulatory regime or institution of reproduction in which a variety of powerful disciplinary practices determine what sorts of bodies should be reproductive and of course, pregnant "addicts" are "off the radar" in this respect. I aim in this chapter to trace the cultural representations of pregnancy and drug use with regards to our "bodily obsessed" society, examine the regulatory regime of reproduction with special reference to pregnancy and drugs and look closely at the "real" material sites or gendered bodies upon which the chaos and disorder of drug use are inscribed.

Given the above, this chapter considers how women drug users whom Nancy Campbell (2000) refers to as "using women", experience reproductive loss (see also Layne, 2003 for a discussion of this concept). I use the concept "reproductive loss" not to conjure up a sense of death and dying but to emphasise that there is certainly a sense of grief and mourning in the "reproductive loss" experienced by "using women". Most importantly, I use the term, "reproductive loss" to emphasise that drug-using women lose or more precisely, are robbed sometimes physically, sometimes metaphorically, through no fault of their own, of their ability to reproduce. This is because, by the very fact of using illegal drugs, these women are seen as socially polluted and not worthy of making babies or being reproductive.

So, reproductive loss for drug-using women is about losing one's reproductive potential in the eyes of society. This is a powerful exclusionary process which targets any woman who uses illegal and sometimes legal drugs and, as a result of this process, women experience a very deep, embodied sense of shame, pollution and social exclusion. Given the above, I want to begin by outlining the structure of the chapter. First, it will briefly challenge traditional assumptions about women in the drug field. Secondly, it will contest the idea that women drug users are polluted. Third and lastly, I look at how, what Tammy Anderson (2005) calls women drug users' core activities, are framed by their feminine and reproductive roles. The aim of the chapter is to answer two questions: "How are we able to contest effectively popular culture's negative views, perceptions and stereotyping of 'using women' as non-reproductive and basically 'shameful'? And "how does an embodiment perspective allow us to mount this contestation?

This is a question that I have been consistently concerned with (Ettorre, 2007a).

Challenging Traditional Assumptions in the Drug Field
For a number of years, the sorrows and joys in the lives of women drug users have remained veiled. Long-established assumptions have been that men are the socially dominant and active subjects in the drug-using culture and women are socially subordinate and relatively passive. While male drug users have been seen to occupy the cultural space of "dominant user", female users have become the targets of societal rage (Kandall, 1996, p. 285). In recent years, these "masculinist" assumptions have been challenged by women scholars (see for example Ettorre, 2007a, 2004, 1992; Measham, 2002; Evans et al., 2002; Raine, 2001; Murphy & Rosenbaum, 1999; Sterk, 1999; Henderson, 1996; and Anderson 1995, 1998, 2005, 2007) within a feminist perspective which develops new types of identities for women (Measham, 2002; Hammersley et al., 2002; Ettorre, 2007b, 2004). For example, Sheila Henderson (1996) suggests a type of sensual hedonism for female drug users whose recreational use is marked by personal agency and pursuit of pleasure. "Feminising drug use" involves considering these women's combined activities such as fashion seeking, clothes consumption, music and dance through a cultural space demarcated by "fun" (Henderson, 1993). Of course, the flip side of this feminisation is demonisation and exclusion particularly in terms of reproduction. Drug-using women are seen by medical experts as shameful, disgusting and unfeminine because they give birth to "addicted babies" (e.g. meth babies, crack babies, etc.). Additionally, because these women use drugs, motherhood is not their right.

Pollution: Questioning a "Contaminated" View
In earlier work (Ettorre, 1992), I spoke of a hierarchy of drugs
implying strong moralising features embedded in the popular
discourse on drugs. Implicit in this hierarchy is the view that
some substances are better as well as more polluting, both
chemically and culturally, than other substances. In a classic
piece, Warburton (1978) defined internal pollution, as the "state
when the security of the internal environment of our bodies is
destroyed". While Warburton noted that internal pollution had
received scant attention in the drugs field at that time, he
argued that it was easy for those with a knowledge of drugs in
society to blame over-prescribing doctors; criticise the
marketing strategies of the pharmaceutical or the alcohol
industry and see the breakdown of governments' attempts to
curb, if not control the illegal global trade in heroin. While
Warburton's ideas are rather outdated, he characterised a
notion which thrives in contemporary society. For him, the
consumers of drugs were to be blamed for internally polluting
their bodies which became the interior environments for
contamination. More importantly, drug users conspired in this
pollution process by insisting on taking drugs. While this
moral judgement was made and drug users were seen to
pollute themselves as well as their social environments, they
involved themselves in a subtle discrimination process.

I would like to translate this view on internal pollution
which still exists today to women drug users. These women are
seen as "polluted women" and they become the main targets in
the above discrimination process. Furthermore, why is it that
female rather than male drug users are targets of this
discrimination process? Mary Douglas has defined pollution as
"a type of danger which is unlikely to occur except where the
lines of structure (i.e., cultural boundaries) are clearly defined"
(Douglas, 1966, p. 113). She suggests these cultural boundaries

33

are more clearly defined for women than for men. Given this, we could argue that the consequence of crossing these boundaries (i.e. polluting their bodies through drugs, becoming out of control, etc.) for women drug users is social exclusion on a grand scale. In a real sense, these women have polluted or soiled identities. Furthermore, pollutants such as drugs are coded as dirt or symbolic matter out of place and as a result, drug-using women can be seen to engage in a state of ritual impurity which is dangerous to self or others and which inheres in certain life events and conditions (i.e. reproduction) (Jewkes & Wood, 1999).

We all know of the low, irreversible status of the female drug user. While women have the disagreeable social function as carriers of difficult emotions, historically they have been punished when these emotions were overstated or they appeared too troublesome (Chesler, 1994). Additionally, in the private/female sphere of domestic life, women, particularly mothers are the primary emotional copers – a reality which has a long term effect on women's psychic lives (Ernst & Goodison, 1997). These social functions and resultant cultural practices have particular consequences for women drug users. Regardless of when, where, how and why women take drugs, they are viewed as having polluted their identities and their reproductive bodies as women. In turn, they have contaminated the private space of family life and the public space of communal cleanliness. In a popular sense, women drug users' bodies are eminently polluted.

Additionally, if she is pregnant, she characterises a body which is "doubly polluted". She is doubly polluted because she consumes illegal drugs contaminating her body in turn, these drugs are seen to have contaminated her foetus. Unlike non-drug using women's bodies, pregnant drug-users' bodies are viewed as lethal foetal containers. Murphy and Rosenbaum

(1999) have shown how pregnant drug users are the focus of social policy concerns and the targets of treatment regimes and the law. Whether their babies are taken from them after birth or they are told to have an abortion, be sterilised or so on, these bodies are viewed as not fit to reproduce. In this context, Carter (2002) contends that women drug users bear three "stigmata" – "they are immoral, sexually indiscrete and inadequate care givers". Furthermore, these stigmata become even more punitive when they use drugs during pregnancy. While the female body is the epitome of women's reproductive nature, drug use is seen as an assault on women's bodies. A drug-using woman becomes the cultural representation of a contemporary woman who does not care enough about her body. Indeed, she is a polluted body *par excellence.*

Women Drug Users' Core Activities through the Lens of Embodied Deviance
Here, embodied deviance is defined as the scientific and lay claim that bodies of individuals classified as deviant are marked in some recognisable way (Urla and Terry 1995, p. 2). Deviant social behaviour always manifests itself in the substance of the "deviant's body". Individuals who deviate from social norms are viewed as socially and morally inferior; their social and moral trouble making is embodied. As a form of "embodied deviance", drug use "marks" bodies of individuals, determining their low status and lack of moral agency. When gender enters the equation we see dramatic results. For example, responsible motherhood is taken away from drug-using women from the perspective of embodied deviance as they are seen to have defiled their bodies with polluting substances: drugs.

Their embodied deviance is all about feminine wilful, self-contamination and all of these ideas are embedded in popular culture. Gendered practices construct the stigmatised drug using female body in such a way that any woman's drug use as a type of female embodiment is disciplined in relationship to others and her reproductive body (Campbell, 1999). Within biomedicine, the symbol of the age of biopower (which is the force producing and normalising bodies to serve prevailing relations of dominance and subordination) is the reproductive body, the body of a woman capable of producing babies under the benevolent guise of medicine. The marking of female bodies as reproductive has been a crucial way in which biomedicine produces and normalises female bodies to serve prevailing gender relations. As women's bodies, including drug-using bodies, are pressed into the service of reproduction, their social agency is defined and valued by how well they reproduce. Of course, for drug users, reproduction is a problematic issue (Murphy & Rosenbaum 1999).

With the above ideas in mind let us look at Tammy Anderson's (1998, 2005) work. Recently she has argued that women appear in the drugs world differently from men and subtle connections between women's pursuits in the illegal and conventional worlds need to be made. Focusing on empowerment and agency, Anderson (2005) contends that women perform four core activities, including (1) providing shelter, housing and other sustenance needs; (2) purchasing goods and services; (3) subsidising or promoting male dependency; and (4) dealing drugs – all fundamental to the social and economic organisation of the drug world (Anderson & Levy, 2003). Anderson sees all of these core activities as embodied activities which are able to aid more conventional lifestyles in future assimilation into the conventional world and are "transferable" to this world. Let us look at each activity from an embodied deviance perspective.

The Domestic Body – Control of the Household
Anderson (2005) notes that one dimension of women drug users' "power" pertains to the housing that drug-using women provide to members of inner-city drug worlds. Calling attention to a woman's control of the household, this activity points to organising the variety of physical, intimate spaces which provide refuge, emotional labour and cultural sustenance for her significant others. For a drug-using woman, she is the domesticated, instrumental and useful body. While many discourses (e.g. biomedical, legal, media, drugs, etc.) regulate her body as a deviant one, there are various technologies of the self (e.g. providing a visible space for significant others, collecting material goods for her and other's subsistence, etc.) at work in her desire for drugs. Perhaps, her domestic and deviant embodiment disrupts dualistic thinking and social norms.

In order to be successful domesticated bodies, women maintain connections between what is viewed by society as their respectable or responsible (e.g. relations with their significant others, such as partner, parental, etc.) and their disrespectful or irresponsible (e.g. drug using) embodied activities. But, criminal justice and medical personnel do not bestow respectability on women drug users even those who are respectable or responsible within their domestic spaces. In the hierarchies of social values and acceptable levels of feminine social conduct (Skeggs 1997, 2004), women drug users remain outside respectability and are more easily classified as dangerous, bad or risky bodies. Gaining respectability while doing drugs is problematic, as shame or disconnection is embedded easily in their domestic lives (Dale & Emerson, 1995). Anderson (2005) notes this core activity provides important forms of capital for women and their dependents enabling successful drug careers. But this success is based on female bodies culturally constructed in opposition to social authority and as a challenge to the continuity of male property and power.

The Consuming Body: Female Purchasing Power
Women drug users are consumers and their ability to raise finances for the purchase of goods and services helps stimulate both illegal and legal economies (Anderson, 2005). Here, I look generally at drug-using women as consumers of drugs and as "powerful economic actors".

In contemporary society, consumer culture is where the reproduction of social inequalities and reinforcement of normality thrives. Consumer culture actively creates the self as of prime importance and orientated towards self-indulgence rather than self-denial (Howson, 2004, pp. 93–4). The consumption of drugs flourishes within a society "addicted itself to the sorry tension between individual excess and social control" (Ferrell & Sanders, 1995, p. 313). While drug use may be viewed as "criminal consumption", designated as deviant and serving mainly male interests or male street cultural capital (Collison, 1996), the consuming body of the female drug user is able to gain competence, control and power (Murphy & Arroyo, cited in Anderson, 2005).

This drug-consuming body is both a cultural construction and social resource. It is constructed by burdensome social and moral discourses. The cultural adages that "drug use is anathema to women's bodies as reproducers" or "women who consume drugs fail in their social responsibility to be the guardians of morals" are refrains emerging from these discourses. Although female users may control economic resources, they may also embody resistance when they break traditional norms by being drug dealers in drug-consuming spaces. This resistance is regardless of the fact that some women may be ill-equipped to handle the violence necessary to maintain their dealing in an environment of security and control (Fagan, 1994).

To consume drugs is to expose one to risk (Collison, 1996). However, the female drug-consuming body creates space for an imaginative form of femininity: criminal pleasures may become escapes from powerlessness and domination inherent in their everyday life.

The Female Labouring Body: Women Subsidising Men's Use

In discussing sources of women's economic power, Anderson (2005) notes that subsidising male drug users, their consumption of drugs, sustenance needs, and lifestyles is a core activity for women users. The female body has no clear or established history and the value put on it has been constant only in so far as it has been constantly less than the value given to the male body (Shildrick, 1997, p. 22). This is true in the drugs field where women's needs are reconstructed as risks and when they are viewed as undeserving of the status "victim" or "citizen" (Malloch, 2004). To see the real value of gendered bodies, especially drug using, female labouring bodies, we must look at these bodies in relation. When women support financially men's drug-using activities, their bodies become "relational resources" whether or not their relationships are marked by risky behaviours (e.g. unsafe sex, drug use, injecting, victimisation, violence or exploitation).

Both female and male users engage in embodied risk relationships and love and intimacy may play a large part in managing these sorts of relationships. For women to be successful as labouring relational bodies, they need to learn about difficult ways of using their bodies and complex, gendered rules of engagement in their intimate relationships. For example, drug-using female sex workers are confronted with not only the risks associated with work relationships but also changing drug fashions (i.e. from crack cocaine, to powder cocaine, to ecstasy, etc.) (Green et al., 2000). They are aware of the risks and benefits associated with these changing drug fashions and the ways different drugs feature in worker, client, manager and dealer relationships. While some drug-using women may thrive economically in this environment, others may become increasingly desperate and find their bargaining power so reduced that they accept a fraction of the money they once received for their services (Willies & Rushforth, 2003). Green et al. (2000) found it was difficult for sex workers to separate professional, work-related from recreational drug use. They experienced their bodies as "occupational resources", shaped by different relationships between "working" and "private" partners, similar to other women who relied on their bodies to produce income (Evans et al., 2002). Here, drugs and risky sex cut across both the public and private boundaries of work and leisure. As labouring bodies supporting partners, female users of all ages, sexual orientations, classes and ethnicities, experience their bodies as relational investments – useful physical capital or resources (Bordo, 1993) similarly to other non drug-using women. Of course, one resource that is somewhat inaccessible as physical capital is reproduction.

The Female Body "In Commerce": Dealing Drugs
The number of women involved in drug selling and their location in the pecking order vis à vis men remain burning issues (Anderson, 2005). When women drug users become engaged in dealing drugs, their bodies are shaped by culture in the commercial world through the business of doing drugs. Bodies are contextualised by gender, race, ethnicity, sexual orientation and class as well as culture. Denton and O'Malley (1999) describe how the illicit drug market is fragmentary and

competitive, lending itself to small business entrepreneurs. They contend that this business structure makes it more practicable for women to succeed in this illicit economy. Furthermore, the lack of a clear authority structure and capacity to absorb new dealers provides fewer barriers for women dealers to overcome. Significant others in women dealers' family networks become a stable operational base for them to be successful drug entrepreneurs. The deviant embodiment of these women reveals a balance between well-disciplined, financially focused bodies and supposedly undisciplined bodies who neglect their families.

Whether or not dealing drugs is an empowering embodied experience (Friedman & Alicea, 2001) for these women, involvement in this activity inevitably has bodily consequences for significant others around them. For example, this is demonstrated by Marilyn, a forty-year-old dealer:

> There was this thing with the Filas [expensive name-brand shoes]. I explained to them [her children], either Mom uses, deals drugs and you have Filas, or I don't use, I'm in treatment and you have Payless shoes. I told them you have a choice … use, don't use
> deal, treatment
> Filas, Payless …
> They chose the Payless shoes. They wanted me around.
> (Friedman & Alicea, 2001, p. 135)

Conclusions

In conclusion then, the female drug using body embodies deviance and is a politically shaped body, formed by practices of control, suppression and restraint. While the construction of "the body" is an effect of endless circulation of power and knowledge, the female drug-using body provides the focus for regulatory practices which target a gendered individual,

41

perceived as a shameful, unfeminine and irresponsible person. A major assumption supporting women's engagement in core activities is that her female body is normalised as life-giver and reproducer. This assumption is taken as a biological given. In our work, we need to challenge this assumption and to win back for women drug users their right to reproduce. Otherwise their lives will continue to be marked by a deep sense of reproductive loss. In answering the question, "how are we able to challenge popular culture's negative views, perceptions and stereotyping of 'using women' as non-reproductive and basically 'shameful?'", we must be sensitive to the sort of reproductive loss using women currently experience.

References

Anderson, T. (1995). Toward a preliminary macro theory of drug addiction. *Deviant Behavior: An Interdisciplinary Journal, 16*(4), 353–72.

Anderson, T. (1998). A cultural identity theory of drug abuse. *Sociology of Crime, Law and Deviance, 1,* 233–62.

Anderson, T. (2005). Dimensions of woman's power in the illicit drug economy. *Theoretical Criminology, 9*(4), 371–400.

Anderson, T. (2007). *Neither villain nor victim: Empowerment and agency among women substance abusers.* Rutgers, NJ: Rutgers University Press.

Anderson, T. & Levy, J. (2003). Marginality among older injectors in today's illicit drug economy: Assessing the impact of aging. *Addiction, 98*(6), 761-70.

Bordo, S. (1993). *Unbearable weight: Feminism, Western culture and the body.* Berkeley, CA: University of California Press.

Campbell, N. (1999). Regulating "maternal instinct": Governing mentalities of late twentieth century US illicit drug policy. *Journal of Women in Culture and Society, 24*(4), 895–923.

Campbell, N. (2000). *Using women: Gender, drug policy and social justice.* New York, NY: Routledge.

Carter C. S. (2002). Prenatal care for women who are addicted: Implications for gender-sensitive practice. *Journal of Women and Social Work, 17*(3), 299–313.

Chesler, P. (1994). *Patriarchy: Notes of an expert witness.* Monroe, ME: Common Courage Press.

Collison, M. (1996). In search of the high life: Drugs, crime, masculinities and consumption. *British Journal of Criminology, 36*(3), 428–44.

Dale, B. & Emerson, P. (1995). The importance of being connected: Implications for work with women addicted to drugs. In C. Burck & B. Speed (eds), *Gender, Power and Relationships* (pp. 168–84). London, United Kingdom: Routledge.

Denton, B. & O'Malley, P. (1999). Gender, trust and business: Women drug dealers in the illicit economy. *British Journal of Criminology, 39*(4), 513–30.

Douglas, M. (1966). *Purity and danger.* London, United Kingdom: Routledge and Kegan Paul.

Ernst, S. & Goodison, L. (1997). *In our own hands: A book of self-help therapy.* London, United Kingdom: The Women's Press Ltd.

Ettorre, E. (1992). *Women and substance use.* Basingstoke, United Kingdom: Macmillan.

Ettorre, E. (2004). Revisioning women and drug use: Gender sensitivity, gendered bodies and reducing harm. *International Journal of Drug Policy, 15*(5–6), 327–35.

Ettorre, E. (2007a). Women, drugs and popular culture: Is there a need for a feminist embodiment perspective? In P. Manning (ed.), *Drugs and popular culture: Drugs, identity, media and culture in the 21st Century.* Cullompton, United Kingdom: Willan.

Ettorre, E. (2007b). *Revisioning women and drug use: Gender, power and the body.* Basingstoke, United Kingdom: Palgrave Macmillan.

Evans, R. D., Forsyth C. J. & Gauthier, D. K. (2002). Gendered pathways into and experiences within crack cultures outside of the inner city. *Deviant Behavior: an interdisciplinary journal,* 23(6), 483–510.

Fagan, J. (1994). Women and drugs revisited: Female participation in the cocaine economy. *The Journal of Drug Issues,* 24(2), 179–225.

Ferrell, J. & Sanders, C. R. (1995). Culture, crime and criminology. In J. Ferrell and C. R. Sanders (eds), *Cultural criminology* (pp. 3–21). Boston, MA: Northeastern University Press.

Friedman, J. & Alicea, M. (2001). *Surviving heroin: Interviews with women in methadone clinics.* Gainesville, FL: University of Florida Press.

Green, A., Day, S. & Ward, H. (2000). Crack cocaine and prostitution in London in the 1990s. *Sociology of Health and Illness,* 22(1), 27–39.

Hammersley, M., Khan, F. & Ditton, J. (2002). *Ecstasy and the rise of the Chemical Generation.* London, United Kingdom: Routledge.

Henderson, S. (1993). Fun, frisson and fashion. *International Journal of Drug Policy,* 4(3), 122–129.

Henderson, S. (1996). E Types and Dance Divas: gender research and community prevention. In T. Rhodes and R. Hartnoll (eds), *AIDS, drugs and prevention: Perspectives on individual and community action* (pp. 66–85). London, United Kingdom: Routledge.

Howson, A. (2004). *The body in society: An introduction.* Cambridge, United Kingdom: Polity Press.

Jewkes, R, J. & Wood, K. (1999). Problematizing pollution: Dirty wombs, ritual pollution and pathological processes. *Medical Anthropology, 18*(2), 163–86.

Kandall, S. R. with the assistance of J. Petrillo (1996). *Substance and shadow: Women and addiction in the United States.* Cambridge, MA: Harvard University Press.

Layne, L. (2003). *Motherhood lost: A feminist account of pregnancy loss in America,* New York, NY: Routledge.

Malloch, M. S. (2004). Not fragrant at all: Criminal justice responses to "risky" women. *Critical Social Policy, 24*(3), 385–405.

Martin, E. (1992). *The woman in the body: A cultural analysis of reproduction.* Boston, MA: Beacon Press.

Measham, F. (2002). "Doing gender" – "doing drugs": Conceptualizing the gendering of drug cultures. *Contemporary Drug Problems, 29*(2), 335–73.

Murphy, S. & Rosenbaum, M. (1999). *Pregnant women on drugs: Combating stereotypes and stigma.* New Brunswick, NJ: Rutgers University Press.

Raine, P. (2001). *Women's perspectives on drugs and alcohol: The vicious circle.* Aldershot, United Kingdom: Ashgate.

Shildrick, M. (1997). *Leaky bodies and boundaries: Feminism, post modernism and (bio)ethics.* London, United Kingdom: Routledge.

Shilling, C. (2005). *The body in culture, technology and society.* London, United Kingdom: Sage.

Skeggs, B. (1997). *Formations of class and gender: Becoming respectable.* London, United Kingdom: Sage.

Skeggs, B. (2004). *Class, self & culture.* London, United Kingdom: Routledge.

Sterk, C. (1999). *Fast lives: Women who use crack cocaine.* Philadelphia, PA: Temple University Press.

Turner, B. (1996). *The body and society* (2nd edn). London, United Kingdom: Sage.

Urla, J. & Terry, J. (1995). Introduction: Mapping embodied deviance. In J. Terry & J. Urla (eds), *Deviant bodies: Critical perspectives on difference in science and popular cultures* (pp. 1–18). Bloomington, IN: Indiana University Press.

Warburton, D. M. (1978). Internal pollution. *Journal of Biosocial Science, 10*, 309–19.

Willies, K. & Rushforth, C. (2003). The female criminal: An overview of women's drug use and offending behaviour. *Trends and Issues in Crime and Criminal Justice,* October 2003, No. 264. Canberra: Australian Institute of Criminology. Retrieved 20 October 2012 from: http://www.aic.gov.au/ publications/

CHAPTER THREE

FOR AN EMBODIED SOCIOLOGY OF DRUG USE: MEPHEDRONE AND "CORPOREAL PLEASURE"

Stephen Wakeman

People think it's all about misery and desperation and death and all that shit, which is not to be ignored, but what they forget is the pleasure of it ...

Mark Renton
(*Trainspotting*)

In his much-cited and much-praised text *The Body and Social Theory*, Chris Shilling (2003) details the "absent present" nature of the body in the genesis of contemporary sociological thought. He infers that while it has been infrequently acknowledged, the body has always maintained a central place in social theory. This line of thought is most resonant in the large array of literature that can be subsumed under the rubric of the sociology of drug use. Throughout this wealth of material, the body is rarely mentioned explicitly, yet always retains a core presence.[1] This is because, quite simply, the effects of drug use are experienced in and through the body – being "high" is an embodied experience. However, I want to expand the idea of the absent presence here; I argue in this chapter that there is another "absent present" in the sociology of drug use that is also inextricably bound to the body – that of *pleasure*. The pleasures of drug use rarely, if ever, receive much attention in social research concerning the use of drugs, neither

---

[1] It is appreciated however that there are some notable exceptions to this claim – they are visited below.

do they figure prominently in policy discourses (O'Malley & Valverde, 2004; Duff, 2008; Moore, 2008). However, the fact that drug use is, for the most part, a pleasurable activity to partake in cannot be ignored. While it is unusual at best to see it take centre stage, it is always there; pleasure – or "corporeal pleasure" (MacLean, 2008) as I will term it below – is an undeniable absent presence in the sociology of drug use. As such, the core concerns of this chapter are to investigate the dynamics of the pleasures of drug use, and then to assess their heuristic and theoretical utility in seeking to account for contemporary changes in patterns of drug use in the UK.

What follows here then is an investigation into the corporeal pleasures of mephedrone use. This chapter has both a theoretical and empirical basis: its main theoretical contention is that "corporeal pleasure" has a unique heuristic quality to it as an analytical concept; and its empirical basis is located in the use of data garnered in an ongoing research project based on the use of legal highs in the UK (Wakeman, 2010). A key problematic revealed early in the project upon which this chapter is based was the peculiarly complex nature of the pleasures associated with the use of these substances, specifically with mephedrone during its journey across the spectrum of legality; its movement from a commercially available legal substance to a prohibited Class B illicit substance. It is argued here that the notion of corporeal pleasure provides a palpable medium through which movements on this scale – that is, the moves made by some drug users from *illicit* to *licit* substances – can be better understood. The chapter opens with a brief introduction to legal highs and mephedrone specifically before moving on to further expound the absent presence of pleasure in both UK drug policy and sociologies of drug use. Following this, recent developments in cultural criminology are mapped out as a possible vehicle through which the analysis of corporeal pleasures can be progressively advanced. In the final section, the narrative accounts of a small group of regular and current mephedrone users are presented to exemplify the theoretical contentions made throughout.

The Rise of Legal Highs and Mephedrone
In March 2010, the then Home Secretary Alan Johnson announced that mephedrone (M-Cat, or meow as it is informally known) and its related compounds were to be banned under the Misuse of Drugs Act 1971 following recommendations from the Advisory Council on the Misuse of Drugs (ACMD) (see Iversen, 2010). Mr Johnson stated: "I am determined to act swiftly on the ACMD's advice and will now seek cross-party support to ban mephedrone and its related compounds as soon as possible." History, it appears, was repeating itself. Just a year previously, the same sequence of events unfolded around a synthetic cannabinoid known as "spice" (see Nutt, 2009); just a year previously again, the stimulant 1-benzylpiperazine (BZP) received the same treatment (see Rawlins, 2008). And now desoxypipradrol, or "Ivory Wave", is set to become the latest link in this chain (Iversen, 2011). It seems that no sooner is one legal high banned, another takes its place. Measham et al. (2010, p. 20) have recently termed this scenario the "cat and mouse" antics that are so indicative of the contemporary "perversities of prohibition". These substances are, prior to legislative measures, bought and sold legally in the UK from many city-centre "head shops" and/or by mail order via the internet. Such substances are produced and consumed solely for their psychotropic effects, despite instructions on their packaging that typically state "not for human consumption" (labels such as this are all that is necessary to bypass restrictions on the sale

of most chemicals in the UK). Mephedrone for example, was frequently sold as "plant feed". There is, however, no evidence to suggest that it has any horticultural utility.

Regarding the prevalence of its use, little is firmly established at present. However, the dance culture magazine *MixMag* claimed in 2010 that mephedrone was the UK's favourite new drug. Based on the findings of their self-report survey, they concluded it was the fourth most frequently used substance overall. In 2011, they found it to be the only substance that did *not* record a fall in use from the previous year. A more authoritative account can be found in the recently released findings of the 2010/11 British Crime Survey (BCS). According to the BCS, 1.4% of 16–59-year-olds, and 4.4% of the 16–24 age group reported mephedrone use within the last year. While these numbers do not appear to be that substantial, they are equal to the numbers for ecstasy and cocaine use respectively (Smith & Flatley, 2011, p. 11). The excellent survey work of Fiona Measham and colleagues tells a similar story: that despite its recent prohibition, and a small decline in reported levels of use, mephedrone still retains its popularity in the UK's night-time economy and beyond (Measham et al., 2011; Moore et al., 2011). Mephedrone provides an unparalleled contemporary example of the well-rehearsed moral panic scenario. In fact, the story began to unfold with an uncanny similarity to Cohen's (1972) classic formulation – the moral barricades were quickly and suitably manned. A search of newspaper websites in the UK revealed 132 articles using the search term "mephedrone" over a twelve-month period spanning 2009/2010.[2] Broadening the term to "legal highs"

---

[2] *The Times* – 20 articles; *The Guardian* – 35 articles; *The Independent* – 29 articles; the *Daily Mail* – 17 articles; *The Sun* – 25 articles; and the *Daily Star* – 6 results.

almost doubled this figure. Stories surrounding this type of drug use frequently featured on the news broadcasts of the UK's main TV stations, and also in the popular Channel 4 show *Hollyoaks*. But perhaps the most startling of these TV appearances came in the form of BBC Three's *Can I Get High Legally?*, a short documentary film in which presenter George Lamb actually took a legal high and described the effects as part of the broadcast.

A closer inspection of these substances reveals strong symbolic and instrumental links with "traditional" controlled drugs. These substances are marketed as being of an equal – or even superior – quality to drugs such as cocaine and ecstasy, and they also share many of their cultural reference points. For example, a search of the many websites selling these products in 2010 revealed the following names of illegal drugs being used for these licit substances: "Pink Champaign" (a type of amphetamine); "Mitseez" and "Doves" (both are common "brands" of ecstasy); "Skullkaps" (a term used to identify potent magic mushrooms); and "Wild Opium".[3] These links are not coincidental, Russell Newcombe's study of mephedrone users in Middlesbrough revealed that over half his sample "explicitly stated that mephedrone's effects were superior to those of cocaine and ecstasy" (2009, p. 11). It seems that the effects of these substances, that is, the *corporeal pleasures* derived from their consumption, are highly valued. As such, mephedrone has, in the space of three or four years, become a core component in many of the "repertoires of distinction" (Measham & Moore, 2009) displayed by contemporary drug users in the UK.

---

[3] See Collin (1998) and Tyler (1995) for more on the branding of illicit drugs in the UK.

The "Absent Presence" of Corporeal Pleasure
With the above considered, the emphasis now shifts to the absent presence of pleasure in the sociology of drug use. Before proceeding any further, it must be noted that "pleasure" is a problematic concept to define in a manner that will be universally accepted. I start here from a conceptualisation of pleasure as being an amalgamation of feelings and sensations brought on by an experience, or the anticipation or memory of an experience, that is both physiologically and socially construed as being "good". True, it is a highly diversified, relative and subjective phenomenon: and to complicate this situation further, notions of pleasure are contingent upon their respective historical, cultural and spatial contexts (see Bloom (2010) for more on the complexities of "pleasure"). Yet, despite concerns around its varying nature, pleasure is undoubtedly an embodied experience – the array of feelings and sensations that can be understood as pleasurable are experienced primarily in and through the body. Thus, in respect of drug use, pleasure and the body are inextricably bound entities. Despite this though, the absent presence of pleasure is more than evident in the field of drug policy and worryingly, from a large proportion of academic research on this subject too. To exemplify this point, a digital search of the ACMD's report to the government on mephedrone and the cathinone compounds (Iversen, 2010), and then the coalition government's 2010 drug strategy reveals that the words "pleasure" and "enjoyment" are entirely absent from both these documents. Moreover, some of the most intelligently argued and insightful academic contributions to the drugs field in recent years make only passing reference to the nuances of the corporeal pleasures of drug use (e.g. Shiner, 2009; Barton, 2011; Seddon, 2010; Stevens, 2011).[4] They are

---

[4] As a notable exception to this rule, see Aldridge et al. (2011).

there, but not there; there is an unspoken assumption regarding the fact that drug use is pleasurable, yet none of these texts devote serious attention to such pleasures or even contain an index entry for the word "pleasure".

In the first instance, this is a stark example of the failure of the UK's government to recognise the pleasures of drug use. In accounting for this failure, O'Malley and Valverde (2004) have noted that activities regarded as "disreputable" are never coded as pleasurable under neoliberal governance. They go on to contend that since the eighteenth century, successive Western governments have ignored pleasure as a motivating factor in deviant activity:

> problematic activities are managed and discussed in ways that deny or silence the voluntary and reasonable seeking of enjoyment as warrantable motives. Governmental discourses about drugs and alcohol, in particular, tend to remain silent about pleasure as a motive for consumption, and raise instead visions of a consumption characterized by compulsion, pain and pathology.
>
> (O'Malley & Valverde, 2004, p. 26)

David Moore (2008) expands this line of thought somewhat and in so doing, neatly accounts for pleasure's absence in social research too. He reasserts O'Malley and Valverde's claim – that there is a political imperative at work in the de-legitimisation of the pleasures of substance use – but importantly adds that there are two other processes active here: (1) a prioritisation of certain forms of knowledge; and (2) a contested social arrangement whereby social bodies have become conceptualised via a "high" or "low" hierarchy (Stallybrass & White, 1986). That is, firstly for Moore (2008, p. 354), "researching pleasure does not generate useful forms of research capital". By this he infers that qualitative research utilising its participant's accounts of the

53

pleasures of drug use is denigrated to a form of "subjugated knowledge" that never fares well in its struggle with the dominant discourse of medicine, the "psy" sciences and epidemiology. And secondly (and plausibly, relatedly), the emergence and continued development of enlightenment-based rationality and liberal socio-economic policies have engendered a conceptual apparatus of "high" and "low" social orders and thus "bodies". There has been, in the Western world, a privileging of the sanitised, rationalised, pleasures of the upper regions of the body (i.e., the head, the spirit, etc.); simultaneously, however, this has permitted and facilitated the discursive formation of the "irrational pleasures" of the lower body – the erotic and sensuous pleasures derived from the fulfilment of "carnivalesque" unruly desires. For Moore, "drugs threaten the liberal body and its disciplined pleasures. They are incompatible with rationality and discipline – contaminating, corrupting, seducing and destroying the will" (2008, p. 356).

Collectively, the above demonstrates the *dis*embodied nature of contemporary understandings of drug use and the drug user. However, recent developments in both feminist and cultural criminology have the potential to reclaim ground here.[5] There is for example, much in the way of congruence between what Elizabeth Ettorre (2007a; this volume) terms a "feminist embodiment perspective", and Jeff Ferrell's "criminology of the skin" that:

> understands and analyzes everyday criminality on the level of pleasure and desire and explores the complex processes by

---

[5] Space precludes a detailed analysis of the feminist theories relevant here – the interested reader is directed towards the excellent works of Elizabeth Ettorre (2007a, 2007b) and Fiona Measham (2002).

> which criminal pressures reproduce, redefine, and resist larger patterns of power, authority, and domination. For pornographers and graffiti writers, drug users and joyriders, the politics of criminality skip across the surface of the skin, and across the many moments of illicit pleasure and sensual excitement that their criminality exudes.
>
> (Ferrell, 1995, p. 316)

Central here are the moments of illicit pleasure; the sensual excitement experienced through the corporeal pleasure of drug use. In seeking to locate the use of mephedrone within this framework, the focus must be on the body, on this phenomenon as it is *actually experienced in its embodied sense*. However, and importantly, it must not be confined to the physiological effects of drug use on the body, as Jack Katz has pointed out in a passage that has become almost *cliché* in cultural criminology: "getting away with something in celebratory style is more important than keeping anything or getting anywhere in particular" (1988, p. 52). Essentially, Katz indicates that there is pleasure to be found in the experience of transgression, not just the reward offered at the end of it. In the present context, there is pleasure to be found in the cultural, stylistic and experiential facets of *being* a drug user, not *just* in the using of drugs. Cultural criminology then is a criminological framework concerned with the experiential features of transgressing laws and moral boundaries – with the lived experiences of deviance (see Ferrell et al., 2004; Ferrell et al., 2008; Hayward, 2004; Hayward & Young, 2004; and Young, 2012 for more on cultural criminology).

In a similar vein, Stephen Lyng contends that the privileging of experience, the pleasures of transgression, are not only resistant in their nature, but corporeal too – they are fundamentally concerned with embodiment:

most aspects of criminal life highlighted by cultural criminology—the pursuit of risk, pleasure, style and empowerment—are ways to "body forth" in a social context where actors are subjected to regimes of work, consumption and communication that deny the creative possibilities of their bodies.

(Lyng, 2004, p. 360)

Lyng's (1990) edgework model – the voluntary pursuit of high-risk activities – also provides a fitting conceptual apparatus through which the study of pleasure can be embarked upon, yet space precludes a greater coverage of this model here.[6] For now though it is hoped that this brief introduction has demonstrated the plausible potential of cultural criminology in the present context. True, this framework has received much in the way of critical attention (see O'Brien, 2005; Farrell, 2010; Hall et al., 2008). Yet, its inherent focus upon style, pleasure, sensation and emotion has all the requisite tools to assist in the formulation of a more embodied sociology of drug use.

For an Embodied Sociology of Mephedrone Use
As indicated above, the following extracts are gleaned from the narrative accounts of a small sample of regular and current mephedrone users in the North- and South-West of England (male and female aged between eighteen and thirty-five). The full methodological details of this ongoing research can be found in Wakeman (2010). For now though, and in brief, all participants were interviewed on at least two separate

---

[6] Essentially, edgework is the term used by Lyng to describe the seeking and undertaking of a risk-based experience in the name of transcending an oppressive social order. For more on this framework see Lyng (1990, 2004, 2005); Lyng et al., (2009); Ferrell et al., (2001); and Reith (2005).

occasions, using an adaptation of Tom Wengraf's (2001) biographic-narrative-interpretive method, across 2009 and 2010. The focus of these interviews was the use of drugs, especially legal highs and mephedrone in relation to whether this type of drug use was primarily motivated by experience or economics – that is, was the move to legal highs representative of emotionally based "thrill-seeking" or rationally based cost/benefit decision-making processes. Again as indicated above, an initial finding and central theme running through all the participants' accounts was the extremely pleasurable nature of mephedrone use. However, these pleasures extended over and above the simple pleasure derived from the psychoactive properties of the substance; mephedrone had unique pleasures to it whilst it retained its legal status. It was found that the users of this substance actually enjoyed acquiring and consuming it legally – that there was a certain amount of pleasure to be found in not having to deal with the constraints of illegality. However, such pleasures and freedoms came at a price, they meant sacrificing another key locus of pleasure – the "pleasures of being bad" (Katz, 1988). It is at this point that this chapter utilises these findings to further its case for an embodied sociology of drug use. The dialectic interplay between these two distinct forms of pleasure firmly establishes the theoretical utility of the concept of corporeal pleasure in the study of drug use and drug-using populations.

Initially, it should be pointed out just how pleasurable mephedrone's use is to some people. The following two short extracts exemplify this point:

> To be honest, when I first done it, I've not found many things that could top that hit y' know?
>
> (Freddy)

> The buzz is great off of it ... it was probably one of the best
> times I ever had in my life.
>
> (Jody)

In a final visit to the ACMD's mephedrone report, some recognition of these experiences and the pleasurable nature of this substance can be discerned, yet as noted above, it refrains from using the "P" word itself. Instead it records in typically scientific fashion "the self reported subjective effects" of mephedrone as: "feelings of empathy (openness, love, closeness, sociability, well-being); stimulation, alertness, and rushing; euphoria, mood lift, appreciation of music; and, awareness of senses" (Iversen, 2010, p. 10). These descriptions are however, devoid of any meaning; they are *disembodied effects* rather than the coded nuances of an embodied experience. An alternative approach identifies a much greater range in the pleasures of mephedrone use – one that transcends its mere "effects":

> I found that mephedrone, it did enhance everything I did, if I
> done something it made it interesting, it made it good, it made
> it fun to do like you know? No matter what that was to be
> honest, walking down the street to the shops, it made it pretty
> cool like.
>
> (Freddy)

Here we can see the wholly embodied nature of mephedrone's use – it provides the user with a means by which the ordinary events of the everyday can be understood and construed of as being pleasurable. There is much in accordance here with Katz (1988, p. 207) who claimed intoxicants to represent "handy, transportable adventure kits – ideally suited for diffusing action throughout one's life".

However, as postulated above, the pleasures of mephedrone use are complex. Pertinent here is the manner in which the substance's legal status impacted upon such pleasures. For example, legality afforded the drug user a somewhat novel experience:

> You didn't have to worry about being banged up for it or whatever, you walk down the road with it in your pocket thinking they can't do nothing anyway so it don't matter, you can even go into a pub and sniff the odd line in front of the barman. He'd have a go at you, then you'd say no, no, it's legal, he'd go, "definitely legal"? I mean, obviously, he can't prove it, but you know, if say for instance you can prove it was what you said it was then he'd go, "oh, alright then". ... Even the old bill like, they pull you over, or they stop you in the street, they find it then they're like, "yeah, we've got one here" like, and you're just stood there laughing ... you're just stood there laughing cus you know they cant do shit!
>
> (Freddy)

Yet, these experiences came at a cost; they were soon realised to be diametrically opposed to an important dimension of pleasure derived from drug use as it is traditionally experienced as an illegal activity. For these men and women, the use of drugs offers an opportunity to embody Katz's (1988) "ways of the badass"; to transgress moral boundaries and to be "bad". In itself, this is a pleasurable activity:

> I think I said something last time about you know, all girls love a bad boy? You know, people love trying to fight the system, especially a system that doesn't work, and if you think in some small little way that you taking drugs is fucking the system then it is attractive. It makes you feel like you've done something a bit naughty, and I don't care who you are,

everybody likes being a little bit naughty at some stage in
their life.

(Robert)

Therefore, we can see that there is a certain amount of pleasure
in being "bad", but paradoxically, in being "good" too – there is
pleasure in the breaking of the law, but also in conducting
oneself in a usual manner yet within the boundaries of the law.
Thus, consideration of the complexities of pleasure is *essential* in
attempts to comprehend this emergent form of drug use.

Through considering Freddy's and Robert's accounts
combined it would be reasonable to introduce more from
cultural criminology's lexicon, namely Ferrell's (1995, 2001)
concept of "resistance". It is plausible to suggest that accounts
such as these demonstrate pleasure in getting one over on the
"system" and its agents of control. Whether or not these young
men and women were acting out of resistance to dominant,
oppressive social orders with true "revolutionary" intent is
unclear, what is clear however is that they *were* doing so, that
they *were* doing so knowingly, and furthermore, that they were
deriving pleasure from the experience too. The use of
mephedrone can be interpreted as a medium through which
these goals and objectives can be embarked upon and partially
achieved. I note "partially" however, because it soon becomes
evident that acting within the boundaries of the law was not
enough here; it did not sustain the resistant, transcendent
project:

It took the fun away. It took that kind of, not being allowed to
do it, y' know? Yeah, just to be able to buy it and not have to
quickly stash it or whatever, you know, under the arm sort of
thing to buy it. You can just go in the shop buy it, walk home,
do it. It's kind of, it's great, cus you can get it really easily,
you know where you can buy it, it's there all the time, but it

took the buzz away from it, the enjoyment of getting the
drugs and not getting caught and that.

(Jim)

For Jim and the others, the pleasures of being bad were lost
through mephedrone's legal status. Whilst this did mean ease
and convenience, it removed the pleasures of *being* a drug user.
While legality had its benefits, it spoiled the experiential basis
of drug use. As cultural criminologists argue, there is a
resistance imperative inherent in some forms of criminality
and/or deviant behaviour – however if the behaviour is then
subsumed into the very system that the actor is resisting, this
dimension of said behaviour becomes lost.

This is where the edgework model demonstrates its
potential in providing the conceptual apparatus required for a
fully embodied understanding of the corporeal pleasures of
drug use. To exemplify this point, we must first consider
Lyng's request of his reader: "[w]e must at least consider the
possibility that people may, on one level, seek a risk-taking
experience of personal determination and transcendence in an
environment of social overregulation" (2005, p. 10). Then
consider this passage from Jim:

> You try to add something to it, because it's like fucking,
> excuse my language, we do as we're told every bloody day,
> get up, do everything we need to do, so when you have got
> something out there that you can just go out and lighten up
> for, just for a day or something, just become something else,
> not become part of this money making world for the richest
> people out there, you need something like that. When you
> can just go and get it that easy, it becomes boring again, so
> you've got to try and like up the stakes and think like, right, if
> I can get it that easy and it's legal then I'm gonna drive whilst
> I'm doing a line, I'm gonna blast me a shottie [a pipe-like

device used for smoking cannabis] while I'm driving the car, you need to just get out of this ordinary world, and that's why we do it.

(Jim)

Jim's behaviour is certainly reminiscent of both the practicalities of "doing" edgework and the emotional desire to engage in such activities too. There can be little doubt that driving a car, whilst not only under the influence of drugs, but actually consuming them at the same time requires considerable "skill". Furthermore, there can be little doubt that Jim's "failure to meet the challenge at hand will result in death or, at the very least, debilitating injury" to use Lyng's (1990, p. 857) definition of the archetypical edgework activity.

Jim's behaviour here pushes the boundaries, his tales of "racking up" lines of mephedrone on the dashboard of his car and snorting them at traffic-light stops reveals his quest to experience the fully embodied feelings of being a "badass", of being a drug user, even though he was consuming a legal substance. As he joked later in the day, "legal or not, you would get in the shit for doing it while you was driving". This is where Lyng's project becomes so central to an embodied sociology of drug use. In seeking and achieving the "edge", in "negotiating the boundary between life and death, consciousness and unconsciousness, ... sanity and insanity" (Lyng, 1990, p. 855), Jim – like all edgeworkers – arrives at a place of "truth". This truth is *corporeal* in its very nature. As Jim is freed from the constraints of "this ordinary world", all he is left with is an acute sense of his fully embodied self. The social world around him fades away as his body and mind – *his very being* – experiences the full spectrum of pleasures available to him in the moment he is in. There is physiological pleasure to be derived from the effects of mephedrone, but in order to attain its experiential pleasure, measures must be taken to transcend its legal status – the corporeal pleasure of mephedrone use is found in the combination of the two. Thus, my argument here is that social theories of drug use *must* recognise the existence and importance of such experiences and that this is only achievable through an increased consideration of the embodied nature of the pleasures associated with drug use. The sociology of drug use must not – as Mark Renton noted in the opening words of this chapter – forget about the pleasures of it.

Conclusions
It is hoped that this short chapter has achieved its aim of highlighting the heuristic utility of corporeal pleasure as an analytical concept in the sociological study of drug use. There is, however, much work still to be done here. The congruence displayed between the theories of cultural criminologists and the experiences of a small sample of mephedrone users clearly shows the potential here for a more nuanced account of the drug user's motivations and proclivities. It must be noted in closing however that there are rightful grounds upon which the above contentions could be criticised. Primarily, "drug use" is a somewhat ambiguous term; though it was used frequently here, it must be recognised that the world of recreational mephedrone use is a very different world to that of the addicted heroin user. Also, the research from which the preceding narrative accounts were gleaned revealed considerable support for cultural criminology's antithesis – the routine activity-based theories of rational choice. There are many who would reject the model of drug use presented here behind a more rationalised character of economic prudence and risk management. However, such concerns need not detract from the overriding claims made in this chapter, namely, that

pleasure can be understood as an absent presence in the sociology of drug use and that cultural criminology, and particularly the edgework model, represents a meaningful avenue through which this absence might be addressed theoretically and empirically in the future.

References

Aldridge, J., Measham, F. & Williams, L. (2011). *Illegal leisure revisited.* London, United Kingdom: Routledge.

Barton, A. (2011). *Illicit drugs: Use and control* (2nd edn). London, United Kingdom: Routledge.

Bloom, P. (2010). *How pleasure works: Why we like what we like.* London, United Kingdom: Vintage.

Cohen, S. (1972). *Folk devils and moral panics* (3rd edn). Abingdon, United Kingdom: Routledge.

Collin, M. (1998). *Altered state: The story of ecstasy culture and acid house* (2nd edn). London, United Kingdom: Serpent's Tail.

Duff, C. (2008). The pleasure in context. *International Journal of Drug Policy, 19*(5), 384–92.

Ettorre, E. (2007a). Women, drugs and popular culture: Is there a need for a feminist embodiment perspective? In P. Manning (ed.), *Drugs and popular culture: drugs, media and identity in contemporary society* (pp. 227–38). Cullompton, United Kingdom: Willan.

Ettorre, E. (2007b). *Revisioning women and drug use: Gender, power and the body.* Basingstoke, United Kingdom: Palgrave Macmillan.

Farrell, G. (2010). Situational crime prevention and its discontents: Rational choice and harm reduction versus "cultural criminology". *Social Policy & Administration, 44*(1), 40–66.

Ferrell, J. (1995). Style matters: Criminal identity and social control. In J. Ferrell & C. Sanders (eds). *Cultural criminology* (pp. 169–89). Boston, MA: Northeastern University Press.

Ferrell, J. (2001). *Tearing down the streets: Adventures in urban anarchy.* Basingstoke, United Kingdom: Palgrave.

Ferrell, J., Hayward, K. & Young, J. (2008). *Cultural criminology: An invitation.* London, United Kingdom: Sage.

Ferrell, J., Hayward, K., Morrison, W. & Presdee, M. (2004). *Cultural criminology unleashed.* London, United Kingdom: Glasshouse.

Ferrell, J., Milovanovic, D. & Lyng, S. (2001). Edgework, media practices, and the elongation of meaning: A theoretical ethnography of the bridge day event. *Theoretical Criminology, 5*(2), 177–202.

Hall, S., Winlow, S. & Ancrum, C. (2008). *Criminal identities and consumer culture: Crime, exclusion and the new culture of narcissism.* Cullompton, United Kingdom: Willan.

Hayward, K. (2004). *City limits: Crime, consumer culture and the urban experience.* London, United Kingdom: Glasshouse.

Hayward, K. & Young, J. (2004). Cultural criminology: Some notes on the script. *Theoretical Criminology, 8*(3), 259–73.

Iversen, L. (2010). *Consideration of the cathinones.* ACMD Report. Retrieved 11 November 2012 from http://www.homeoffice.gov.uk/acmd1/acmd-cathinodes-report-2010?view=Binary

Iversen, L. (2011). *Consideration of desoxypipradrol (2-DPMP) and related pipradrol compounds.* ACMD Report. Retrieved from: http://www.homeoffice.gov.uk/publications/drugs

Katz, J. (1988). *The seductions of crime.* New York, NY: Basic Books.

Lyng, S. (1990). Edgework: A social psychological analysis of voluntary risk-taking. *The American Journal of Sociology, 95*(4), 851–86.

Lyng, S. (2004). Crime, edgework and corporal transaction. *Theoretical Criminology, 8*(3), 359–75.

Lyng, S. (ed.) (2005). *Edgework: The sociology of risk-taking.* London, United Kingdom: Routledge.

Lyng, S., Matthews, R. & Miller, W. J. (2009). Existentialism, edgework, and the contingent body: Exploring the criminological implications of ultimate fighting. In D. Crew & R. Lippens (eds), *Existentialist Criminology* (pp. 94–126). London, United Kingdom: Routledge.

MacLean, S. (2008). Volatile bodies: Stories of corporeal pleasure and damage in marginalised young people's drug use. *International Journal of Drug Policy, 19*(5), 375–83.

Measham, F. (2002). "Doing gender" – "doing drugs": Conceptualising the gendering of drug cultures. *Contemporary Drug Problems, 298*(2), 335–373.

Measham, F. & Moore, K. (2009). Repertoires of distinction: Exploring patterns of weekend polydrug use within local leisure scenes across the English night-time economy. *Criminology and Criminal Justice, 9*(4), 437–64.

Measham, F., Moore, K., Newcombe, R. & Welch, Z. (2010). Tweaking, dabbing and stockpiling: The emergence of mephedrone and the perversity of prohibition. *Drugs and Alcohol Today, 10*(1), 14–21.

Measham, F., Wood, D., Dargan, P. I. & Moore, K. (2011). The rise in legal highs: Prevalence and patterns in the use of illegal drugs and first- and second-generation "legal highs" in South London gay dance clubs. *Journal of Substance Use, 16*(4), 263–72.

MixMag. (2010). *Mephedrone: Meet the UK's favourite new drug.* Information retrieved 28 March 2010 from: http://www.mixmag.net/words/news/mephedrone%3A-meet-the-uks-favourite-new-drug .

Moore, D. (2008). Erasing pleasure from public discourse on illicit drugs: On the creation and reproduction of an absence. *International Journal of Drug Policy, 19*(5), 353–8.

Moore, K., Measham, F., Østergaard, J., Fitzpatric, C. & Bhardwa, B. (2011). *Emerging drug trends in Lancashire: Focusing on young adults' alcohol and drug use.* Lancashire Drug and Alcohol Team. Retrieved 11 November 2012 from: http://www.ldaat.org/

Newcombe, R. (2009). Mephedrone: The use of mephedrone (m-cat, meow) in Middlesbrough. *Lifeline Publications and Research.* Retrieved 21 January 2012 from www.lifeline.org.uk

Nutt, D. (2009). *Consideration of the major cannabinoid agonists.* ACMD Report. Retrieved 6 June 2010 from: http://www.homeoffice.gov.uk/publications/drugs

O'Brien, M. (2005). What is *cultural* about cultural criminology? *The British Journal of Criminology, 45*(5), 599–612.

O'Malley, P. & Valverde, M. (2004). Pleasure, freedom and drugs: The uses of "pleasure" in liberal governance of drug and alcohol consumption. *Sociology, 38*(1), 25–42.

Rawlins, M. (2008). *Control of 1-benzylpiperazine (BZP) and related Compounds.* ACMD Report. Retrieved 6 June 2010 from: http://www.homeoffice.gov.uk/publications/drugs

Reith, G. (2005). On the edge: Drugs and the consumption of risk in late modernity. In S. Lyng (ed.), *Edgework: the sociology of risk-taking* (pp. 227–46). London, United Kingdom: Routledge.

Seddon, T. (2010). *A history of drugs: Drugs and freedom in the liberal age.* Abingdon, United Kingdom: Routledge.

Shilling, C. (2003). *The body and social theory* (2nd edn). London, United Kingdom: Sage.

Shiner, M. (2009). *Drug use and social change: The distortion of history.* Basingstoke, United Kingdom: Palgrave Macmillan.

Smith, K. & Flatley, J. (2011). *Drug misuse declared: Findings from the 2010/11 British Crime Survey.* London, United Kingdom: Home Office.

Stallybrass, P. & White, A. (1986). *The politics and poetics of transgression.* London, United Kingdom: Methuen.

Stevens, A. (2011). *Drugs, crime and public health.* London, United Kingdom: Routledge.

Tyler, A. (1995). *Street drugs: The facts explained, the myths exploded.* (2nd edn). London, United Kingdom: Coronet.

Wakeman, S. (2010). Style or substance, flair or function? A critical evaluation of rational choice theory and cultural criminology with recourse to their epistemological and methodological viability in the study of legal high use. Unpublished MA dissertation: University of Chester, Chester, United Kingdom.

Wengraf, T. (2001). *Qualitative research interviewing.* London, United Kingdom: Sage.

Young, J. (2012). *The criminological imagination.* Cambridge, United Kingdom: Polity.

CHAPTER FOUR

WHY CRITICAL DISABILITY STUDIES?

Dan Goodley

In this brief essay I want to explore the focus of this book – Corporeality: the body and society – and ask why critical disability studies? What has critical disability studies to offer studies of bodies and their place in society? I seek to expand on some recent writing (Goodley, 2011) and directly address the questions through reference to the potential of critical disability studies to speak about, with, and sometimes against bodies and society. If (late) twentieth century disability studies were associated with establishing the factors that led to the structural, economic and cultural conditions of the exclusion of people with sensory, physical and cognitive impairments, then critical disability studies in the current century might be seen as a time of developing nuanced and sophisticated theoretical responses to these conditions. The politicisation of disabled people is at the heart of these developments. Disability activisms have brought about a host of national and pan national responses including the *UN Convention on the Rights of Persons with Disabilities*. The potency of *Disabled People's International* is testimony to the growing interconnectedness of the politics of disability across the globe. On the ground, disability studies have entered a host of training and educational contexts, policies and professional practices. Furthermore, disability studies have dallied with many theoretical ideas. This is not simply about academic curiosity (though some might ask what is the problem with curiosity). Critical disability studies start with disability but never end with it: disability is *the* space from which to think through a host of political, theoretical and practical issues that are relevant to all (Goodley, 2011).

Contemporary disability studies occupy and agitate for what Carol Thomas (2007) defines as a transdisciplinary space: breaking boundaries between disciplines; deconstructing professional/lay distinctions and decolonising traditional medicalised views of disability with socio-cultural conceptions of disablism.

Real?

Why critical disability studies? Well, this is a good question. In an excerpt from David Simon's (*The Wire*) new HBO (Home Box Office) series *Treme*, which premiered in the United States on 11 April 2011, focusing on life and survival in New Orleans, one of the key characters suggests that in order to rebuild the city universities need to produce engineers, not graduates of women's studies, queer studies and black studies. While disability studies is, as per the norm, never mentioned, implicit within the statement is a suspicion of studies that appear to emphasise identity over structure, discourses over materiality and academia over activism. The tension appears to be around the usefulness of disability studies and its status as a worthy area of research, learning and knowledge generation. Just as broken cities need to be physically rebuilt by surveyors, structural engineers, architects and builders, so the logic goes, impaired bodies (and minds) require the input of medics, psychologists, physiotherapists and other medically oriented professions. Critical disability studies are often considered as outside the real realm of possibilities provided by medicine and science to the body. I do not share these suspicions but want to keep the tensions hanging around. "Why disability studies?" is a question being increasingly asked not simply by those outside of the arena but within it. Indeed, in a recent Blogspot, the disability activist and writer Tom Shakespeare castigates those disability studies researchers and writers who engage in theory generation rather than empiricist research:

> Why, then, do so many social scientists prefer to generate theory, rather than to search for evidence? The UK sociologist Ian Craib once described social constructionism as a form of social psychosis. Rather than engage with the world as it is, too many academics would rather deconstruct the terminology people use. He called this a manic defence. People will argue about boundaries and labels, but I would rather be realist about disability. The best way to interpret the evidence is to say that impairments exist. People with impairments generally have problems, partly generated by those impairments, and partly generated by the way societies fail to respond adequately to those impairments.
>
> (Shakespeare, 2011, n.p.)

In a book entitled *Corporeality: The Body and Society*, one could argue that the contributors – and the editors, of course – are recuperating the power of the academy, of social sciences and humanities, moving our focus away from the real problems of bodies. Instead, if we follow Shakespeare (Tom, not the other famous writer), then this book – and this chapter, of course – moves away from the real dilemmas of bodies and embraces instead the shallow contributions of social theory. I do not share this view. I do, though, want to ask, "why critical disability studies?", and offer some tentative, hopefully affirmative answers which display the contributions of theory to the realities of living with a body in the world.

Activism
Why critical disability studies? Because *disability activists and their organisations demand* ideas to be generated that help us all

71

understand disablism. Critical disability studies provide theoretical, empirical and practical resources to aid or – at the very least – parallel the politics of disability. There are, of course tensions and these should not go away. Some activists worry about disability politics becoming safe and domesticated by academia through the development of disability theory, disability studies curricula and disability studies courses. Others view critical disability studies as the place through which to magnify the conditions of disablism, which we can define following Thomas (2007) "as a form of social oppression involving the social imposition of restrictions of activity on people with impairments and the socially engendered undermining of their psycho-emotional well being". Disablism occurs at the macro level of structural discrimination and is to be found in useless anti-discriminatory legislation, inflexible employment laws and exclusionary educational policies and practices. These structures aid the sifting and sorting of different bodies into "able and willing" and "disabled and needy". But disablism is also felt relationally, psychologically and subjectively. Stares, inappropriate comments, the fascination of non-disabled people are often endured by disabled people: to the extent that these responses get "under the skin" and threaten to injure, psychologically scar and invalidate.

Why critical disability studies? Because there is an *epidemic of signification* around the disabled body and psyche which threatens the death of disability. When Fanon (1993, p. 112) writes a "racialised epidermal schema is one in which I was battered down by tom-toms, cannibalism, intellectual deficiency, fetishism, racial defects, slave ships" this leads us to consider the processes of medicalisation, psychologisation and pathologisation wrapped up in the making of disabling epidermal schema. Paul Gilroy (2009) draws upon Fanon to call for a renewed engagement with the human after the "death of wo/man" brought about by the conditions of racism. To this we can add disablism. Critical disability studies theory can and must unpick and deconstruct the various ways in which discourses of impairment, abnormality and deficiency are increasingly being generated about bodies and minds. This is not simply an interesting pastime of a cultural studies theorist; it is an essential theoretical retort to the unproblematic ways in which more and more discourses of the body are being written on to the body. When a body is covered and marked by pathological discourses then pathology is inevitably felt by the body.

Why critical disability studies? Because of this *neoliberal capitalist world* we live in that threatens to (re)affirm the idealised fully functioning, responsible, reasonable individual body and demonise the monstrous Other. Weiss (1999, p. 164), following Rosi Braidotti (1994), defines this ideal self – this big phallic subject – as "reasonable man": as "man-white-western-male-adult-reasonable-heterosexual-living-in-towns-speaking-a-standard-language". In contrast other bodies are captured by terms such as "suffering from", "afflicted by", "persistent vegetative state", "the mentality of an eight-year-old", "useless limb", "good and bad leg", "mentally unstable", "deranged" and "abnormal" (Olkin, 2009, p. 17). Disabled people become Other: the absolute other crossed through (Rose, 1986). And the neoliberal ideals have massive implications for our treasured institutions. Haraway's description of school written in 1991 has clear resonance:

> School: deepening coupling of high-tech capital needs and public education at all levels, differentiated by race, class and gender; managerial classes involved in educational reform and refunding at the cost of remaining progressive

> educational democratic structures for children and teachers;
> education for mass ignorance and repression in technocratic
> and militarized culture.
>
> (Haraway, 1991, p. 171)

Never has critical disability studies been more necessary.

Governance

Why critical disability studies? Because we live in a time of *governing our souls* that calls out to us to tend obsessively to our bodies, to fight death and erase those aspects of life we deem vulnerable, incomplete and challenging. The politics of life itself, for Rose (2001), is an ontological politics – a political life caught up in ontological obsession, confession and self-help. A good friend of mine, a consultant neurologist, swears by a recently acquired self-help text entitled "How to survive your partner's ex-wife and support his children". This is a cultural signifier of the politics of life itself: the nightmare described by Michel Foucault (1991) that we are free but free only to govern ourselves. And we know when self-absorption is the name of the game then the Other is paradoxically distanced (made more Other) and kept closer (through attempts to govern the Other).

Psychologisation

Why critical disability studies? Well forgive the personal beef here but because *psychology exists and is proliferating*. My own university location – amongst psychologists and psychologies – might explain this preoccupation but there are clearly problems with the growing psychologisation of life. Naughty boys have ADHD. Children that play in a solitary fashion exhibit autistic tendencies. Children that fail to adapt to the pressures of schooling display oppositional defiance disorder. Linked to

Rose's (2001) point about the politics of life itself, it is crucial that critical disability studies challenges institutional and professional practices that psychologise the conditions of oppression faced by those of a non-normative persuasion. Psychology loves its non-normates and has a host of diagnostic classifications lying in wait ready for the ambush. We are told by the American Psychiatric Association that "Publication of the fifth edition of *Diagnostic and Statistical Manual of Mental Disorders* (DSM-5) in May 2013 will mark one the most anticipated events in the mental health field". They are not wrong. Read the document and you will find "Oppositional Defiant Disorder" a label being increasingly applied to kids who disrupt neoliberal classrooms (and not to psychologists, funnily enough). You will find revisions to the classification of "Premenstrual Dysphoric Disorder" which includes symptoms such as:

(1) Marked affective liability (e.g. mood swings; feeling suddenly sad or tearful or increased sensitivity to rejection)

(2) Marked irritability or anger or increased interpersonal conflicts

(3) Markedly depressed mood, feelings of hopelessness, or self-deprecating thoughts

(4) Marked anxiety, tension, feelings of being "keyed up" or "on edge"

(5) Decreased interest in usual activities (e.g. work, school, friends, hobbies)

(6) Subjective sense of difficulty in concentration

(7) Lethargy, easy fatigability, or marked lack of energy

(8) Marked change in appetite, overeating, or specific food cravings

(9) Hypersomnia or insomnia

(10) A subjective sense of being overwhelmed or out of control
(11) Other physical symptoms such as breast tenderness or swelling, joint or muscle pain, a sensation of bloating", weight gain.

I am reminded of the feminist view in the 1990s that PMT, as it was then known, should be viewed as an opportunity for women to be incensed with patriarchy at least once a month. Instead, we are entering a period of time where psychologisation is not only growing but spreading in a rhizomatic fashion across the globe – infecting all who meet it (see Hardt & Negri, 2000).

Materiality
Why critical disability studies? Because *disability is materially everywhere yet nowhere*. We know disability works as a prosthetic – a cultural crutch as Mitchell and Snyder put it – a signifier for deviance, the exotic, the scary, the fascinating. We hear disability spoken, shouted in schoolyards (2005). My nine- and ten-year-old daughters tell me that "spaz" and "queer" dominate the schoolyard put-downs. Yet neither queer theory nor disability studies enter their school curriculum. We know from the new *World Report on Disability* from the World Health Organization (2011) that one billion people live with impairments: the biggest minority group (though I do worry about this one-upmanship around who's got the biggest majority). But do they live only as cultural vents? As signifiers of lack? We know that hate crime against disabled people is on the increase; that disabled children continue to be excluded from mainstream education; that disabled people are often poor.

Why critical disability studies?   Because of the need to engage *disability studies with other transformative agendas*.   As Mitchell and Snyder (2005) put it, disability finds itself in a peculiar situation in the academy: it is allied with a form of subaltern knowledge that is disparaged and sought after at the same time.   Disability is subjected to a form of compulsory feral-isation as defined by Mitchell and Snyder (2005); it is made to stand out as feral in nature. But equally disability studies must connect with critical race, feminisms and queer theories because, historically, it has not.

Onwards – Conclusions

Why critical disability studies? Well why indeed? This is a crucial question that we should never cease from asking. When critical disability studies believes that it knows all the answers to this question then it is dead. Indeed, in Britain, there have been times when some of our leading disability studies researchers seem to imply (or clearly state) that new research is meaningless; that new theoretical developments are irrelevant and not applicable; that critique is getting in the way of ideas that are ready to be employed. This certainty around disability studies can only create a self-referential disability studies that loses touch with the complexity of social, cultural and political life.   Rather, disability studies provides a space – just like feminist, queer, critical race, class studies – where we grapple with the hidden dangers of ideology.

Rosa Luxemburg's most famous formula for revolutionary thinking was "Freedom is always the freedom to think otherwise" (see Rose, 2011). We can only hope that critical disability studies adopts a similar formula: maintaining, following Paul Gilroy (2009), an uncomfortable reflexive position on the conditions and causes of marginalisation. Here then is a rationale for the development of social theories around the body and society. Our task must be to continuously question taken-for-granted ideas around the body. To be suspicious of new languages of the body that seek to pathologise bodies and individualise the problems of living with an Other body in a society that denigrates any deviation from the norm. To make connections across transformative arenas of queer, feminist, postcolonial, critical race and class studies. To locate the body as already a body produced in and by a society, culture and community. To explore the ways in which living in and with a body might offer possibilities for resistance: for new ways of embodiment; new forms of corporeality that refute the pincer-like groups of societal norms. To imagine modes of production – societal, economic, cultural and embodied – that might offer the chance of connections between bodies. Critical disability studies might offer one such place to start developing these theoretical agendas.

References

Braidotti, R. (1994) *Nomadic subjects: Embodiment and sexual difference in contemporary feminist theory*. New York, NY: Columbia University Press.

Fanon, F. (1993). *Black skins, white masks* (3rd edn). London, United Kingdom: Pluto Press.

Foucault, M. (1991). *Discipline and punish: The birth of the prison*. London, United Kingdom: Penguin.

Gilroy, P. (2009). "Multiculture, cosmopolitanism and conviviality". Public lecture, University of Manchester, 5 July 2011.

Goodley, D. (2011). *Disability studies: An interdisciplinary introduction*. London, United Kingdom: Sage.

Haraway, D. (1991). *Simians, cyborgs and women: The reinvention of nature*. London, United Kingdom: Free Association Books.

Hardt, M. & Negri, A. (2000). *Empire.* Cambridge, MA: Harvard University Press.

Mitchell, D. & Snyder, S. L. (2005). Compulsory feral-ization: institutionalizing disability. *PMLA, 120*(2) 627–34.

Olkin, R. (2009). *Women with physical disabilities who want to leave their partners: A feminist and disability-affirmative perspective.* California, CA: California School of Professional Psychology and Through the Looking Glass, Co.

Rose, N. (2001). The politics of life itself. *Theory, Culture & Society, 18*(6), 1–30.

Rose, J. (1986). *Sexuality in the field of vision.* London, United Kingdom: Verso.

Rose, J. (2011). What more could we want of ourselves! [Review of the book *The letters of Rosa Luxemburg,* by Adler et al]. *London Review of Books, 33*(12), 16 June 2011, 5–12.

Shakespeare, T. (2011). When realism is critical. Blog for the Nordic Network of Disability Research. http://nndr.org/2011/11/21/when-realism-is-critical/ Accessed 25 November 2011.

Thomas, C. (2007). *Sociologies of disability, "impairment", and chronic illness: Ideas in disability studies and medical sociology.* London, United Kingdom: Palgrave.

Weiss, G. (1999). The duree of the techno-body. In E. Grosz (ed.), *Becomings: Explorations in time, memory and futures.* (pp. 161–75). New York, NY: Cornell University Press.

World Health Organization. (2011). *World Report on Disability.* Geneva, Switzerland: WHO Press.

CHAPTER FIVE

SURVEILLANCE OF THE LEAKY CHILD: NO-BODY'S NORMAL BUT THAT DOESN'T STOP US TRYING

Cassandra A. Ogden

Leakiness is a word often associated with accidental loss (I have a gas leak), a form of dysfunction (my tap is leaking) and occasionally used to describe an intentional disclosure of secret information (an employee was responsible for the leak). When an object or being "leaks" they are losing something, e.g. valuable energy, liquid or information that they once held and that object or person is then left lacking in some way. Leakiness in relation to the body is generally viewed as a symptom, a result of our body failing in some manner or at best, failing to control. When using "leakiness" in relation to the body and bodily fluids the term may appear repugnant and distasteful, a reminder that as humans we are corporeal as well as thinking beings. This chapter utilises the term leakiness to aggravate and discomfort readers whilst interrogating social experiences of leakiness. It will highlight the construction of the "normal" (non-leaky) body as something that is unobtainable and almost always misleading. A non-leaking body is something that is desirable and preferable to contemporary society as it aids functionality, reduces embarrassment and creates the illusion of control (a victory of wo*man* over nature). Through the example of experiences of children with Inflammatory Bowel Disease (IBD) the myth of the non-leaky body will be deconstructed and challenged and the extent to which bodies are controlled elucidated.

Our obsession with bodies within the Western world is apparent when we consume any medium of communication. "Perfect" bodies (normalised aestheticism) are brandished on advertising boards, within magazines, newspapers, films and television screens and emulated within everyday life by modification of bodies through make-up, dieting, exercising, styling and surgery to obtain as close to the "ideal" bodily forms as possible. The concept of the "ideal" bodily form is fluid, taking different forms both between and within cultures, nevertheless for many decades the physical capital obtained from possessing an "aesthetically pleasing" body has been enough to encourage both men and women to turn to the surgeon's knife. The cultural focus upon the body within contemporary Western societies is concentrated around its aesthetical properties whilst the functionality of the body is largely ignored (unless a body is obviously "dysfunctional" and then enters a dialogue which usually renders these bodies "abnormal" or "deviant" and thus in need of medical intervention). Until fairly recently, the embodied experiences of living were largely ignored by sociologists, before authors such as Bryan Turner (1984) and Chris Shilling (2003) began writing on the topic of corporeality and the sociology of the body was born. The body is now an accepted area of study within sociology as well as other social science disciplines where embodied elements of living require attention, exploration and elucidation. Despite this, direct explorations of some of the most mundane and rudimentary aspects of living (i.e. defecating, belching, sneezing, coughing, urinating) tend still to be disregarded as embarrassing realities of life which warrant little sociological attention. Articles on such topics are limited within the sociological field (with the exceptions of Pickering, 2010 and Lundblad and Hellstrum, 2005), despite the proliferation of papers that can be found amongst medical, psychological and biological journals. Biomedicine holds the monopoly on the discussion of such matters and due to its increasing surveillance of the body and diagnoses of bodily performance, the fiction of the "normal" body is created. Due in part to medicine's and allied professions' work, ableism (Campbell, 2009) operates at every level of life and in this instance serves to pathologise bodies unable to control bodily fluid. It is important that sociology obtains a position in discussing bodily functions, to highlight the social aspects and implications of defecating, belching, urinating, etc., and the socially constructed nature of "the non-leaking" body.

Experiences of living with IBD can be applied to key concepts utilised in the sociology of the body and critical disability studies literature that suggest how leakiness has been constructed, how certain discussions about leakiness are legitimated (whilst others stigmatised) and how the creation of abnormal leaky "others" serve to construct an idea of an unobtainable, normalised, non-leaky body. IBD is a term used to refer to at least two other chronic diseases, Crohn's disease and ulcerative colitis. Some patients are diagnosed with indeterminate colitis when it is not possible to distinguish between the two. Those diagnosed with IBD will experience inflammation somewhere along their gastrointestinal tract which will make the area painful, hot, swollen and red (Drossman et al., 1991). This inflammation causes symptoms ranging from diarrhoea and abdominal cramps to a loss of appetite, and chronic fatigue. In ulcerative colitis the patient is more likely to experience bloody diarrhoea due to inflammation localised in the colon. There are a number of extraintestinal manifestations of IBD but for the purpose of this chapter it is the diarrhoea which is of most significance. Although symptoms can be alleviated with medical intervention (nutritional therapy, drugs or surgical intervention), there is no known cure for the disease and those with IBD will experience periods of remission and relapse at unknown periods in their lives.

It is worthwhile to note how this chapter has chosen to initially introduce IBD. A biomedical understanding is assumed to legitimise some shared ontological reality of all people identifying with the label "IBD". Yet the paradox exists that as biomedicine serves to normalise bodies and behaviours which "others" and stigmatises anyone outside that norm, it also offers those who are "othered" by their own medical diagnosis the only possibility (in Westernised societies) to maintain or achieve some degree of normalcy. Thus biomedicine has both the power to classify and survey (with the support of various administrative functionaries), whilst also benefiting from the glory of being able to diagnose and alleviate suffering. Yet this is not the result of a plot to classify, discriminate and obtain power but more of a symptom of discursive formations built on ideals of scientific rationality and the modernist pursuit of advancement over nature through science. As part of a wider questionnaire-based study which asked 100 children with IBD about all aspects of their lives (Ogden, 2006), the narrative inquiry technique was utilised to interview two children with IBD (and one of their mothers) about their experiences of living with this disease (extracts of which will be utilised throughout this chapter). A number of individuals choose to resist labels given to them by medical professions but the people within this study accepted the label and the validity of the biomedical explanation of their bodies. On one occasion the mother of a child with IBD described a time when she challenged the medical experts' diagnosis of her son, but quickly justified this as a period of denial. The biomedical definition of IBD therefore needed to be elucidated to identify one aspect of the reality of living with IBD from the respondents' perspective.

Research conducted on the issue of children with IBD has tended to be *about, rather than with the children*. Macphee, Hoffenberg and Feranchak (1998) highlighted how IBD could potentially act as a key disruptor towards independence which is strived for amongst children with IBD and deemed a healthy aim by authors. Much research on children with IBD has further focused on coping, with many studies centring on the idea of adaptive and maladaptive ways of coping (e.g. Engstrom, 1991; Gitlin et al., 1991; Van der Zaag-Loonen et al., 2004). Such literature highlights the importance of obtaining independence in terms of disease control whilst deeming coping behaviours, such as avoidance or submission to the disease, to be negative. Searching for an individualised problem inherent in the "patient" to understand the children with IBD further locates them firmly within biomedicine. Whilst all focus is upon the individual the studies fail to appreciate the externally situated problems which serve to impact negatively upon members of this population's lives, such as ableist agendas that serve to individualise, pathologise and normalise.

Although in the past, literature about IBD was exclusively written from biological or psychological perspectives (Ogden, 2010), papers have also tried to ascertain the social impact of having IBD. Empirical studies discuss how some children with IBD are dissatisfied with their body image (Decker, 2000; O'Brien and Bridget, 1999), experience social impairment due to diarrhoea making it difficult to leave the house or play with friends (Akobeng et al., 1999; Moody, Eaden & Mayberry, 1999) or how IBD affects attendance or performance at school (Akobeng et al., 1999; Moody et al., 1999; O'Brien and Bridget, 1999). A more recent study has shown how perceived stigma can have a negative effect on the psychosocial well-being of patients with IBD (Taft et al., 2009). Therefore it is recognised that the symptoms of IBD can be disabling but due to the nature of these studies the cause of the disablement appears to lie within the nature of the disease or the inability of individuals to cope with it. A sociological exploration of IBD comes close only through the work of Kelly (1986), who talked of his own experience of living with ulcerative colitis. Nevertheless a theoretical explanation of his experiences was not offered and thus a theoretical sociological study of IBD is still absent.

Norbert Elias's work *The Civilising Process* (1994) shows how thresholds of shame and repugnance help shape the modern conception of manners and deny the reality of bodies. His approach looks towards the history of society and manners and exposes the social nature of individuals within it. Underpinning the work is Elias's belief that sociology needs to fully appreciate the interdependence of individuals to help truly understand society and those within it. Much of his work concentrated on exposing the Western myth of the human as closed and individualised (*homo clausus*) and in advancing his view of the open and interdependent individual (*homines aperti*) (Elias, 1994). In *The Civilising Process* (1994) Elias studied historical books on manners (that later became books of etiquette) and showed how ideas about etiquette have developed over hundreds of years. In the Middle Ages, for example, certain bodily practices like blowing one's nose and defecation were not met with disgust but were regarded as "normal" parts of everyday life. Bodily fluids were "allowed" to be seen and people removed mucus from their nose by removing it with their fingers and throwing it to the ground (to be trodden on immediately). It was not until the eighteenth century that handkerchiefs were used and to gaze at the product was deemed disgusting (Elias, 1994). Defecation was not discussed much in the texts he studied and there seemed to be only one formality surrounding the act; to not engage in conversation with someone who was in the act. Defecation was otherwise just a natural, unashamed part of life, people would refer to it openly and it did not happen in assigned places so it was suggested that "before you sit down, make sure your seat has not been fouled" (Elias, 1994, p. 110).

The practices surrounding defecation in the Middle Ages may seem rather uncivil to many in today's society, at best perhaps unhygienic, and many may find it difficult to see any merit in this society at all. On the whole we appear much more civilised and seem better able to free ourselves from the constraints of our impulses. By considering how society might react to a person showing the symptoms of IBD during the Middle Ages, it may help to better understand how social attitudes towards and amongst people with bowel problems are formulated in contemporary society. Although it is only possible to rely on speculation, a person with IBD in the Middle Ages could be further stigmatised due to the public nature of defecation rendering the "culprit" known and knowable. It appears through Elias's accounts (1994) however that matters of defecation are neither extraordinary or worthy of conversation. Perhaps the public "knowledge" of the variety of faeces renders no one an expert (except everyone) and makes the construction of "normal" faeces less possible. Our civilised nation with private, flushable toilet systems, ensures individuals need not touch or even look at *their own* faeces (let alone anyone else's) and would not dream of entering the bathroom when someone else is vacating the toilet. Our knowledge of faeces comes primarily from the only people who have to know about such matters, the medical professionals. We know individuals with IBD are "abnormal" because they are rendered as such by the fact they are given a label by biomedicine. Biomedicine's job is to find the faults and fix them "normally" functioning bodies are not their patients (although ideas of normalcy are what drives and informs their practice). Through the medical gaze (Foucault, 2003) a person with IBD is "known" (at least by themselves and the professionals) and is expected to gain help with symptoms through biomedicine. The biggest social decision is left untouched (perhaps the most difficult factor) and the "patient" is to decide independently whether or not to "disclose" this seeming negative attribute to the rest of the world. As Taft et al. (2009) noted, it is the perceived stigma that leads to psychological harm to the person with IBD more than the enacted stigma. A closed society such as ours encourages individuals to contain their actions and thoughts especially if they are deemed deviant or undesirable. The merits of elements of the Middle Ages lifestyle is not in some "perverse" desire to see other people's excrement but in living in a society which does not take exception, or try to deny the reality of such a natural part of life. By closeting off certain corporeal activities we serve to contribute once more to the idea of *homo clausus*, the myth of the independent self. As Elias explains (1994) the process of civilisation is so socially situated that we naturalise our response to dealing with human action and fail to realise that our practices are socially constructed.

Elias (1994) regards the Renaissance as the period when the compulsion to check our own behaviour was tightened, in a similar way to Foucault (1991) regarding the Enlightenment as the period when increased discipline and surveillance entered society under the guise of greater efficiency and rational thinking. Elias explains that although the ways we deal with our most basic bodily functions are regarded as common sense today, once they were considered elaborate rituals. When we go to the toilet in our bathroom, behind a locked door, we do not have a sense of conforming to a system of shared norms constructed over hundreds of years because we *want* to go to the toilet in private and hygienically. The privatisation of defecation is not natural but a result of practices enforced upon societies for a number of years. It appears more civilised than previous systems but it comes at a cost. The privatisation of matters leads to individualisation and secrecy, further contributing to misunderstanding that informs ignorant beliefs and ideas. Such beliefs manifest themselves as negative stigma in the lives of children with IBD which cause some to feel shame and embarrassment about their bodies.

Our acceptance of leaky bodies presents itself on a continuum in contemporary society. We do for example expect and accept leakiness at both the beginning and end of life whereas during the period of independence people are expected to be more controlled. Babies are dependent for all things until they grow old enough to be able to control their own urges. Elias alludes to how children are conditioned by their family to learn the rules of society:

> young people have only two alternatives: to submit to the pattern of behaviour demanded by society, or to be excluded from life in "decent society". A child that does not attain the level of affect-moulding demanded by society is regarded in varying gradations from the standpoint of a particular caste or class, as "ill", "abnormal", "criminal" and "impossible", and is accordingly excluded.
>
> (Elias, 1994, p. 120)

Many developmental theories, books and internet sites exist to assure parents or guardians that their child is developing "normally". A key identifier of developing "normally", "effectively" and "efficiently", is the ability for toddlers to be potty trained. Governmental handbooks are distributed to every mother in the United Kingdom on the development of children, designed to help parents and guardians bring up their child "successfully". Such publications contain apparently "important" statistics on the percentage of children "dry" at certain ages (Welsh Assembly Government, 2007) which promotes the idea of "normal" bowel and bladder control. Adapting Foucault's work on biopower (1990) it appears that observing, recording and disseminating knowledge about the body serves to formulate discourses of normalcy which pathologise and stigmatise those who display "otherness". Bodies that excrete differently, more profusely or frequently are not just "othered" but are repugnant "others". Tremain (2002) adopts a Foucauldian analysis to understand the socially constructed nature of both disability and impairment and shows how the creation of nation states helps further homogenise and normalise bodies. Bodies are merely articulated within discourse and impairment and therefore Tremain may argue that IBD is far from ontologically real but a construction of biopower. The more we know about bodies (healthy or otherwise) the more they can be surveyed and the bigger belief in "natural" (normal) reality, the greater the ability for institutions to expand regulatory effects. Society knows the average age that children learn to go to the toilet themselves, this knowledge is then used to normalise that process, rationalise and medicalise it. The person with IBD requires (and desires) the medical gaze as their body appears "other" to normality and serves to infantalise their body as it cannot be controlled. A person engages with the technologies of self (Martin, Gutman and Hutton, 1988) by adapting behaviour, concealing thoughts and changing behaviour to create the illusion of normality within their own bodies. It is desirable to reduce the effects of being "different" (anything other than "normal", which is unachievable anyway) and medicine offers a range of ways to reduce the symptoms of disease, hence the negative effects of biomedicine's work (in terms of labelling and surveillance) remains concealed.

Amongst the children with IBD interviewed and surveyed, a range of similar issues were raised that highlighted the presence of biopower in their lives. One theme that persisted in children's responses to questionnaires was the idea of "hiding" their IBD from others (with 65% (n=61) of respondents, claiming they had hidden their IBD to some extent (Ogden 2006)). Katey and Nathan also discussed the different degrees of "hiding" their disease:

> I am determined to go to school again tomorrow though. I am able to hide it for the moment from everyone else, although it really kills when I am on the toilet.
>
> Katey (aged 13)

> To help me cope with having the disease I take a mixed approach really. Firstly, I don't try to hide my IBD (this is why I have told some of my closest friends). At the same time I don't go around bragging about it like I am someone special! I think by telling everyone that I had IBD would make it harder in the long run and might mean that certain nasty people would bully me.
>
> Nathan (aged 11)

Both respondents discussed how their close family members knew about their IBD and a handful of other close friends, although they only told people they trusted in case they got teased or bullied. The idea of being different or even disgusting because of their IBD was prevalent in the questionnaire study (with 54% (n=52) of respondents reporting they felt embarrassed because of their IBD) and also evident within the narratives.

> I am so scared of going out with this abscess [situated on the anus and a symptom of her IBD] because I don't want to leak all the badness on my clothes. Mum and Dad are trying to get me to go out but they don't know how embarrassing it would be if I leaked.
>
> (Katey)

The idea of avoiding accidents in order to maintain a degree of normality was also articulated by Nathan's mother, Clare:

> we didn't really go that far in those years, we led quite a close life. I became very conscious of where the loos were situated you know, in Asda or Morrisons wherever we were doing our shopping. It was worth it though to save Nathan from feeling dirty or different.

Control over where to go as a family and how to get there was pertinent to controlling the symptoms of IBD for Clare and she was trained in knowing how to prevent any "embarrassing" situations that could arise from having an accident. Much illness work was performed in order to obtain the idea of normalcy. A similar focus was discussed in Lundblad and Hellstrum's (2005) work which highlighted how Swedish school children aged thirteen to sixteen years were most likely to avoid using school toilets due to their negative perceptions of them (physical appearance, offensive smell and/or feelings of insecurity). These perceptions meant children would prefer to experience physical discomfort rather than the psychological and social discomfort experienced if they used the school toilets. Avoidance of embarrassment attached to defecation and urination is not therefore exclusive to a pathological few. Defecation and urination has been individualised to such an extent that children and young adults are made to feel embarrassed about going. This study demonstrates how the problem has been partially created by poor provision and thus can be partially addressed outside the body, nevertheless the extent to which shame is felt upon and within the body has not been elucidated.

In *The Contours of Ableism,* Campbell (2009) highlights how regimes of ableism are apparent within a number of societies and refers to the insidious nature of internalised (and thus naturalised) ableism. In the lives of those who are deemed "different" or "abnormal" it is assumed that the desire for normalcy is paramount (and it usually is due to the power of ableism). As "normality" is never truly defined, even those who are not explicitly "othered" may engage in practices to help them achieve "hyper-normality". The ableist project as Campbell (2009) suggests will only ever promote sameness and will always denigrate the experience of disability (or otherness by way of chronic illness). The way of "dealing" with disability is therefore to integrate, cure and eliminate. Children with IBD are therefore not failing to cope by hiding their disease from the rest of the world or in some state of denial but are acting rationally to the ableist agenda as they feel deviant being different. If we do as Campbell suggests and use the ableist lens to gaze not upon the impaired for once but on the ableist regime, one can see more clearly how normalising processes of defecation practices serve to stigmatise and pathologise. It may serve to encourage children with IBD to deny the ontological reality of their bodies or at best be ashamed by it.

> He copes with it well, he will say "Mum I am just going to have a shower now", or even just gets one by himself. He cleans the basin out and sorts himself out. I think that the less attention that I draw to it, the better, so it just becomes normal to him.
>
> Clare (mother of Nathan)

In this excerpt the mother wishes to normalise the IBD within her son by showing how having diarrhoea is manageable and could be solved practically. This process of "normalising" her child's difference is once again a rational response regarding current discursive understandings of difference. The notable lack of language such as "acceptance of difference" is interesting. Allowing her son to achieve independence in controlling his IBD is also notable which relates closely to ideas of privacy and containment, perhaps with the ultimate aim as passing as "normal". Campbell's work highlights not just the presence but also the myth of ableism. Children negotiating their IBD know that all bodies are leaky but that their bodies in time of relapse are more so. During the life course bodies are differently leaky with common colds and flus increasing leakiness and making it more difficult to control. Leakiness is sometimes a result of a positive life experience, but despite the cultural obsession with sex, society remains particularly silent or prudish about the act's leaky realities. Without the intense surveillance of "abnormal" bodies, the normal body could never be imagined. With regimes of discipline encouraging the surveillance of self, the fiction of the non-leaky controlled body is born, despite its unrealistic claims. Regardless of the commonality of leaky bodies, society ensures that leakiness is kept behind closed doors (preferably locked).

Shildrick (1997) and Foucault (1990, 1991, 2001, 2003) further enable a sociological exploration of the phenomenon of leakiness as both authors deconstruct the normativity of bodies and the site of power and the body. Biopower has been introduced previously through the work of Tremain, however another important aspect of biopower is the power of the confessional (Foucault, 1990). Foucault describes current discourse as encouraging people to talk about themselves and, whilst being subjected to powers that force confessions, people simultaneously believe that they can only know themselves through the confessional. The people to whom confessions about IBD are more likely to be disclosed are doctors and allied health professionals. The discussion of matters of the bowel to health care professionals may even feel liberating for children with IBD with the hope for alleviation of symptoms or even cure. Despite this liberatory potential, it appears through the above quotes that children with IBD will only confess to a select few and therefore this truth finding exercise is only partial in their lives. Furthermore, help from the health professionals will allow children's bodies to be further controlled biomedically and the need to confess to others is reduced. According to Foucault (1990) the idea of the confessional as liberating is a mere social construct which leads to and could be deemed as coercion. In this sense gastroenterologists' observations, and classifications of and interventions with/for the child with IBD contributes to a further distinction of an "other". These processes are what contribute further to the project of normalcy which further constrains and stigmatises the experiences of having IBD; thus partially through the confessional, people themselves become part of the order that subjects.

This chapter has discussed the issue of leakiness literally whereas Shildrick (1997) uses the idea of leakiness to describe how body and society leak into each other highlighting the myth of the biological reality of the body. In being critical of the modernist (gendered) project of a fixed body and related fixed identity, Shildrick (1997) believes a feminist ethic will develop which will allow embodied selves to become valued. Bodies are discursively formulated and through postmodern feminism, bodies' boundaries can be better seen as shifting and leaky. Simplistic dichotomies between "normal" and "other" bodies therefore need to be broken down as no-body can conform to the idea of normalcy. Shildrick's use of the term "leaky bodies" is provocative and of particular relevance for this paper. There is no better example of Shildrick's concept of a leaky body than a body that leaks excessively and uncontrollably (at times). When a body cannot control some of its basic functions the embodied realities of life come to the fore. People's "common sense" notions of civil behaviour, the pursuit of rationality and productivity over corporeality are shaken when bodies are leaky and transcend people's notions of control. Overtly leaky bodies assist Shildrick's conceptual leakiness to deconstruct clearly contained categories and fixed ways of being and transgress the myth of normalcy.

This exploration of children with leaky bodies (those with the label of "inflammatory bowel disease") highlights some of the ways in which children are encouraged to control their motions, despite living their lives through bodies which make this difficult. A diverse range of sociological theories has emphasised the discursive creation of such bodies and how they are situated, classified and ranked in a late-modern society. It appears the main difficulties in experiencing IBD as a child/young adult lies not so much in the physical symptoms themselves (medical professions are able to alleviate such suffering) but in the social negotiation which appears necessary to feel accepted by others. In the quest to achieve "hyper-normality" every person in society surveys themselves and to ensure achievement of this standard must also survey others around them. Biopower allows for the creation of the ultra-controlled, normalised (and fake) non-leaky body whilst ableism sustains and contains damaging ideas of normalcy.

This analysis of regimes of surveillance inherent in society suggests a need for change to contemporary society's hegemonic ideals of civility and normality, so that difference of any nature can be accepted. As ideas of civilisation are so naturalised, the shift towards a "de-civilising" process that serves to account for embodied experiences of life and appreciates the interdependent nature of individuals seems improbable. Sociologists have nevertheless managed to provide certain theoretical tools to enable abolishment of the myths of independent, self-sufficient, static bodies. Through the discussion and acceptance of the reality of diarrhoea and other bodily fluids, the leaky boundaries of imagined bodies can truly be realised. Only by turning the analytical lens towards the non "othered" will a space be negotiated that allows for open acceptance of everyone and the language of difference and normalcy will no longer be required.

References

Akobeng, A., Suresh-Babu, M., Firth, D., Miller, V., Mir, P. & Thomas, A. (1999). Quality of life in children with Crohn's Disease: A pilot study. *Journal of Pediatric Gastroenterology and Nutrition, 28*(4), s. 37–9.

Campbell, F. K. (2009). *Contours of ableism.* Basingstoke, United Kingdom: Palgrave Macmillan.

Decker, J. (2000). The effects of Inflammatory Bowel Disease on adolescents. *Gastroenterology Nursing, 23,* 63–6.

Drossman, D., Leserman, J., Li, Z., Mitchell, M., Zagami, E. & Patrick, D. (1991). The rating form of IBD patient's concerns; a new measure of health status. *Psychosomatic Medicine, 5*(6), 701–12.

Elias, N. (1994) *The civilising process.* Oxford, United Kingdom: Blackwell.

Engstrom, I. (1991). Family interaction and locus of control in children and adolescents with Inflammatory Bowel Disease. *Journal of the American Academy of Child and Adolescent Psychiatry, 30*(6), 913–20.

Foucault, M. (1990). *The history of sexuality: An introduction, Vol.1.* London, United Kingdom: Penguin.

Foucault, M. (1991). *Discipline and punish: The birth of the prison.* London, United Kingdom: Penguin.

Foucault, M. (2001). *Madness & civilization: A history of insanity in the Age of Reason.* London, United Kingdom: Routledge.

Foucault, M. (2003). *Birth of a clinic: An archaeology of medical perception.* London, United Kingdom: Routledge.

Gitlin, K., Markowitz, J., Pelcovitz, D., Strohmayer, A., Dorstein, L. & Klein, S. (1991). Stress mediators in children with Inflammatory Bowel Disease. In J. Johnson & S. Johnson (eds) *Advances in Child Health Psychology* (pp. 54-62). Gainesville, FL: University of Florida Press.

Kelly, M. (1986). The subjective experience of chronic disease: Some implications for the management of ulcerative colitis. *Journal of Chronic Diseases, 39*(8), 653-66.

Lundblad, B., & Hellstrom, A.-L., (2005). Perceptions of school toilets as a cause for irregular toilet habits among school children aged 6-16 years. *Journal of School Health, 75*(4), 125-8.

Macphee, M., Hoffenberg, E. & Feranchak, A. (1998). Quality of life factors in adolescent Inflammatory Bowel Disease. *Inflammatory Bowel Disease, 4*(6), 6-11.

Martin, L. H., Gutman, H. & Hutton, P. H. (1988). *Technologies of the self: A seminar with Michel Foucault.* Amherst, MA: University of Massachusetts Press.

Moody, G., Eaden, J. & Mayberry, J. (1999). Social implications of childhood Crohn's disease. *Journal of Pediatric Gastroenterology and Nutrition, 28*(4), s. 43-5.

O'Brien B. K. (1999). Coming of age with an ostomy: Life with a stoma may be especially difficult for teens. *American Journal of Nursing, 99*(8), 71-6.

Ogden, C. (2010). Potential of narrative inquiry approach in developing a psychosocial understanding of Inflammatory Bowel Disease (IBD) in children: An essential addition to health related quality of life (QoL) instruments? *The International Journal of Narrative Practice, 2*(1), 57–71.

Ogden, C. (2006). Quality of life and coping amongst children and adolescents with Inflammatory Bowel Disease. Unpublished doctoral dissertation. University of Central Lancashire, Preston, United Kingdom.

Pickering, L. (2010). Toilets, bodies, selves: Enacting composting as counterculture in Hawai'i. *Body and Society, 16*(4), 33–55.

Shildrick, M. (1997). *Leaky bodies and boundaries: Feminism, postmodernism and (bio) ethics.* London, United Kingdom: Routledge.

Shilling, C. (2003). *The body and social theory* (2nd edn). London, United Kingdom: Sage.

Taft, T. H., Keefer, L., Leonhard, C. & Nealon-Woods, M. (2009). Impact of perceived stigma on Inflammatory Bowel Disease patient outcomes. *Inflammatory Bowel Disease, 15*(8), 1224–32.

Tremain, S. (2002). On the subject of impairment. In L. J. Davis (ed.), *The disability studies reader* (pp. 32–47). London, United Kingdom: Continuum.

Turner, B. (1984). *The body and society* (1st edn). London, United Kingdom: Sage.

van der Zaag-Loonen, H., Grootenhuis, M., Last, B. F. & Derkx, H. (2004). Coping strategies and quality of life of adolescents with Inflammatory Bowel Disease. *Quality of Life Research, 13*(5), 1011–19.

Welsh Assembly Government, (2007). *Birth to five.* Cardiff, United Kingdom: Welsh Assembly Government.

CHAPTER SIX

MERCENARY KILLER OR EMBODIED VETERAN? THE CASE OF PAUL SLOUGH AND THE NISOUR SQUARE MASSACRE

Paul Higate

In recent years, the exponential growth of the Private Militarised[1] and Security Company (PMSC) sector into a multi-billion dollar global industry has provoked two main responses. The first is broadly sympathetic and stresses the benefits of the market in regard to the industry's abilities to respond flexibly to rapidly changing security conditions within the context of stabilising post-conflict countries such as Iraq and Afghanistan. The second response to the industry has been one of considerable unease, typically expressed by critical scholars, commentators in the Non Government Organisation (NGO) sector, and at the time of writing, the Karzai government in Afghanistan and the al-Maliki government in Iraq. Here, there is general agreement that a loosening of the state's monopoly on violence is a retrograde step as it unleashes a market for force (Avant, 2005) that thrives on insecurity and its accompanying distortions, as well as denying local people employment because of the influx of expatriate security personnel. In support of this more critically inclined view,

---

[1] I prefer the word 'militarised' to 'military' (as in Private Military Security), since it is more attuned to the core beliefs shaping social practice in the industry (see Enloe, 2002, pp. 23–4 on 'core militaristic beliefs').

private security contractors'[2] perpetrations of human rights abuses are frequently invoked, underscoring the belief that, somewhat paradoxically, the PMSC sector *exacerbates* the insecurity of host populations. The killing of seventeen Iraqi civilians – including children, men and women – in Nisour Square in Iraq in 2007 by five members of a Blackwater personal security detail (PSD) is a case in point. It is against the immediate backdrop of the Nisour Square massacre that the following discussion is set. Its main aim is to go beyond explanations for the killings that focus on the background and pathology of the perpetrators as men of a particular kind. Rather, through foregrounding the most high profile of the perpetrators, Paul Slough, it seeks to complement current explanations with the situational and embodied dimensions of the incident.

The chapter is organised as follows. First I provide some background to the killings, before going on to show how Slough was constructed through a good man/bad man binary as explanation for his role in the massacre. Discussion then shifts to theoretical concerns drawing on the work of interactionist sociologist Randall Collins whose model of a forward panic is applied to the incident in Nisour Square. Third, I apply a phenomenological sensitivity to the genesis of military embodiment as one way in which to account for the brutality of violence perpetrated more widely in military atrocities. Fourth, the implications of foregrounding military embodiment are considered in regard to questions of responsibility, with a focus on the relevance of particular forms of habituated social practice. A brief conclusion follows.

---

[2] Abbreviated to 'contractors' in the remainder of the article.

Background: The Nisour Square Massacre

> "Don't shoot please!" Khalaf recalled yelling. But as he stood
> with his hand raised, Khalaf says, a gunman from the fourth
> Blackwater vehicle opened fire on the mother gripping her
> son and shot her dead before Khalaf's and Thiab's eyes. "I
> saw parts of the woman's head flying in front of me" Khalaf
> says, so many shots had been fired at the car from "big
> machine guns" that it exploded, engulfing the bodies inside in
> flames, melting their flesh into one.
>
> (Cited in Scahill, 2007, p. 5)

It is just after midday on 16 September 2007 in Nisour Square in
Baghdad. Seventeen Iraqi citizens, including children, lie dead
and dying amongst the smoking ruins of burning vehicles
ripped apart by large calibre weaponry used by contractors of
the US PMSC, Blackwater.[3] Another twenty are wounded, the
screams of onlookers and victims' relatives pierce the cordite-
heavy air. It is a scene of utter carnage.

An investigation carried out on 17 September by the US
military cast doubt on Blackwater's plea of self-defence, that
they responded in line with their rules of engagement after
coming under attack from small arms fire and a vehicle borne
improvised explosive device (VBIED). Further details of the
shootings emerged. Witnesses describe how members of the
team opened fire indiscriminately and with no justification. It
was also reported that a Blackwater contractor drew his
weapon on a team member in order to stop him firing as the
command of "cease fire" went unheeded (Scahill, 2007, pp. 3–9).
This incident followed numerous others where local people had
been shot, injured and sometimes killed by contractors on

---

[3] In an attempt to shake-off its deteriorating image, the company
changed its name to *Xe Services* in 2009 and then to *Academic* in 2011.

convoy protection duties as their vehicles got too close.[4] As the sense of shock and trauma was replaced with anger and frustration, explanations for the massacre were demanded. How could so many people have been killed in a shooting spree that lasted a full fifteen minutes? What was the reason for the use of disproportionate force or overkill – where, quite literally, thousands of rounds of ammunition were expended against what appeared to be an unsubstantiated threat?

Dominant Explanations for the Killings

Media attention quickly focused on Paul Slough, a member of the Blackwater PSD believed to be the first to open fire and the main shooter in the incident (Scahill, 2007, p. 33). He provided a sworn statement the day after the killings, excerpts of which are included here:

> On 17th[5] September 2007 at approximately 1230 hours, team 23 deployed out of checkpoint 12 in direct support of team 4's return ... as our motorcade pulled into the intersection I noticed a white four door sedan driving directly at our motorcade ... I and others were yelling, and using hand signals for the car to stop and the driver looked directly at me and kept moving toward our motorcade ... I shouted and engaged the vehicle until it came to a stop.

Slough's statement was thoroughly discredited by witnesses and it was concluded that the PSD had not come under attack. During the trial of the Blackwater contractors on 19 January 2008, *The New York Times* Saturday Profile focused on Paul Slough in an article entitled "From Texas to Iraq, and Centre of

---

[4] See Chatterjee (n.d.).
[5] The spelling and typographical errors made by Slough remain as per the original document (including the incorrect date).

Blackwater Case" (see Thompson, 2008). Its aim was to counter Slough's demonisation in the immediate aftermath of the killings through posing the question of how it was that a former soldier with an unblemished military record could be involved in this internationally notorious massacre. Excerpts from the *New York Times* article follow:

> I went on 20 to 30 missions with Paul. You could always depend on him ... He was always careful. He was always professional. I never knew him to break the rules of engagement.
>
> Several people ... said problems with alcohol made it difficult for Mr Slough's father, Paul Slough Sr, to hold a steady job. They said the younger Mr Slough grew up quickly.
>
> Mike Norrell, Mr Slough's former teacher at Patton Springs School, recalled Mr Slough as a boy who craved learning.

Slough was described as an honourable, decorated military veteran, another said "Mr Slough had not become some kind of cowboy, high on adrenaline and quick on the trigger" (Thompson, 2008). Taken together, these comments attempted to humanise the contractor with their legitimacy derived from the people that had witnessed Slough growing up. Here Slough was not some kind of hypermasculine killer, rather he was a hapless victim of a challenging mission. The subtext to this understanding concerned the realities that faced Slough and his team on 16 September, challenges that were beyond the comprehension of most ordinary people who had never experienced the dangers of an Iraq boiling over with a determined and lethal insurgency. Here was a team of highly trained US veterans working in a hostile environment where, three years earlier, four of their Blackwater colleagues had been lynched by a bloodthirsty mob whilst immobilised by traffic (see Patterson, 2009).

Presented in ideal-typical terms, two explanatory narratives can be identified. First was that generated by the industry's detractors, where contractors were typically viewed as hypermasculine cowboys, intent on killing and injuring Iraqis for whom they were believed to have contempt at best, and a racist disregard at worst. Second, and to counter this, Slough's defenders sought to underscore his professionalism through invoking his triumph over adversity. While this second understanding does allude to the structural or contextual exigencies influencing security work in this environment, both narratives rely heavily on a psychologistic or individualistic explanation for the killings. Taken together they are constitutive of a bad guy/good guy binary with the latter seeking to humanise Slough. What were his experiences of growing up in Dickens and what can be said about his family dynamics, given the early loss of his principal male role model? In presenting Slough in this way there is at one and the same time an attempt to both rehabilitate the perpetrator and dilute his responsibility for the killings.

That both narratives centre on the man behind the incident mirrors dominant explanations for a wide range of violent incidents, from serial killing[6] to that of concern here – a militarised massacre. High profile cases involving military or militarised killings have sparked debate around soldiers' backgrounds and the ways in which their brutal and brutalising experiences provide for spill-over violence (Baron et al., 2006

---

[6] Illustrative in the British context is the "Yorkshire Ripper" Peter Sutcliffe, whose background and "pathology" was endlessly discussed in the popular media for a considerable period after his imprisonment for murdering thirteen women.

Melzer, 2002). Is it any surprise that individuals trained in violence within a culture of aggression should be disposed to killing and injuring unarmed civilians? Yet, using military masculinity or militarised masculinity as unquestioned explanatory variables (Rosen et al., 2003; Jeffreys, 2007)[7] can help to occlude alternative lines of enquiry.[8] These can be opened up by asking questions around women's use of violence,[9] as well as those men with the *same*[10] backgrounds and experiences of perpetrators who do *not* use violence on return from a combat zone, military operations, or as veterans working in militarised roles. What can be said about this largely unacknowledged cohort, members of whom constitute the majority? Why is it their backgrounds and pathologies as masculine men fail to engender violence? What of the myriad, unconsidered acts of restraint exercised routinely by hyper-masculine soldiers and veterans working in similarly onerous

---

[7] Though there can be little doubt that particular branches of armed forces foster misogynistic and aggressive hypermasculinity, yet these co-exist alongside a plurality of military masculinities (Higate, 2003).

[8] A related question is raised by Stephen Tomsen who questions the implied causal links between excessive alcohol intake and violence when he states: "Plenty of very drunk patrons did not get involved in arguments and fights" (Tomsen, 1997, p. 94).

[9] Ongoing research into the Democratic Republic of Congo's national army found that female service members framed themselves as considerably more violent than their male peers, including their self-reported role in sexualised violence (personal communication Dr Maria Baaz-Eriksson).

[10] Of course, it could be argued that no two individuals can have "the same experience", yet background is often invoked at a high level of generality, for instance in the current examples, "soldiers" and "veterans", identities that are seen to contain the generative seeds of violence.

environments (see Higate, 2012)? In addressing these questions, it is helpful to complement the extensive literature emphasising background and pathology with a consideration of the very particular *situational* characteristics of violence – a point to which discussion now turns.

Pathways to Violence: Situational Contingencies and Interactional Chains

Taking my analytic cue from the interactionist sociologist Randall Collins, I argue that causes of atrocities, massacres or put differently in regard to the specific case of Nisour Square – overkill – is only *weakly* correlated with pathology, culture or background as typically noted in normative uses of the term hypermasculinity. Approaches that provide scope for examining the immediate context of violent social practice complement the role and salience of background with the situational construction of actor meaning and subsequent action (Tomsen, 1997, p. 91). Collins argues that violence is far more difficult to carry out than is commonly believed,[11] and in providing a specific definition of violence[12] notes that individuals with a diversity of class, race, age and socio-economic backgrounds perpetrate violence. Explaining causes of violence in this way counters pathologised understandings of

---

[11] For example, Collins identifies the significant gap between empirically observed violence and so-called "entertainment violence", the latter of which is accorded significant influence in shaping perception since, not least, directly observed violence is rare.

[12] Collins' definition of violence is absolutely central to the line of argument developed here. His concern is with "physical violence ... which has a clear core referent", to be distinguished from that of "symbolic violence" that lacks the "situational contingencies" of the former (Collins, 2008, p. 24).

violent individuals, or what Collins (2008, p. 84) notes is the "dependent variable [in the case of Paul Slough, an aggressive hypermasculinity] ... after the fact", where backgrounds are relentlessly scrutinised for evidence of the violent actor, interpreted to fit the violent act *post facto*.[13] As an alternative to focusing on Slough as either a good man or a bad man, Nisour Square might be more persuasively explained using Collins's model of a forward panic which is characterised by patterned interactional chains where tension and fear are translated into extreme violence and senseless overkill, particularly against those who are unable to defend themselves – the hallmark of the Nisour Square massacre.

Nisour Square as Forward Panic
Collins argues that:

> A forward panic starts with tension and fear ... it has a dramatic shape of increasing tension ... the tension/fear comes out in an emotional rush ... they [the perpetrators] are in an overpowering emotional rhythm, carrying them on to actions that they would normally not approve of in calm reflective moments
>
> (Collins, 2008, p. 85)

With this in mind, Paul Slough's sworn statement also contained the following lines:

> Fearing for my life and the lives of my teammates, I engaged the driver and stopped the threat ...

> Fearing for the gunner's life, I engaged the vehicle and stopped the threat ...

---

[13] These processes are akin to a schema, the most influential sociological analysis of which is to be found in Smith's discussion of a "mentally ill" female (Smith, 1978).

> Fearing for my life, I engaged the suspect vehicle in order to stop the threat

Since the veracity of Slough's account was challenged, this particular fearing vocabulary of motive should be treated with caution (Collins, 2008, p. 337), yet it cannot be entirely dismissed in light of the observation that the contractors' bodies were trapped in the confined space of the easily identifiable Sports Utility Vehicles (SUVs). Much like the Marine Lt Philip Caputo, a soldier desperate to extricate himself from a US helicopter touching down in a hot landing zone in Vietnam, similarly Slough and his team experience their SUVs as "enclosed space ... [evoking] a sense of total helplessness ... claustrophobia ... in the small space: the sense of being trapped and powerless ... is unbearable" (Collins, 2008, p. 82). Adrenaline is starting to surge in the SUVs. The mood in the vehicles is volatile. Fingers seek reassurance in the smooth metal of triggers. An explosion is heard and Slough fires first. He is rapidly followed by the others, some of whom may have mistaken Slough's outgoing rounds as incoming enemy fire. Following their military drills and training, remaining team members fire in the general direction of the perceived threat and the shooting continues relentlessly. The Blackwater team may "feel a blind fury [or in this case at least, frustration] toward the forces that have made [them] powerless ..." that in turn, is transformed into:

> A fierce resolve to fight ... but this resolve ... cannot be separated from the fear that has aroused it ... all a soldier can think about is the moment when he can escape his impotent confinement and release the tension ...
>
> (Collins, 2008, pp. 83–5)

In the course of a forward panic perpetrators are blind to their relative power in the use of violence where weakness of a victim "does not matter ... even if they [the perpetrators] are explicitly aware of it" (Collins, 2008, p. 91). Forward panics involve hot emotions and emotional contagion and as Slough opens up with his weapon, the Blackwater team become entrained in the shared interactional solidarity of their firing, as:

> more often the process is group entrainment in a collective emotion ... the Bam! Bam! Bam! of the guns is also part of the rhythm they are caught up in ... being together [provides for] moods to feed off each other ... and keep them locked into their frenzy.
>
> (Collins, 2008, p. 93)

The violence has an immanence all of its own and appears both irrational and morally reprehensible to stunned and bewildered onlookers. The defining feature of a forward panic is overkill and the use of force far beyond what is needed and firing far more bullets than is necessary (Collins, 2008, p. 94). Witness the Blackwater team's shooting of individuals in the back, the killing of children, cars riddled with thirty or even forty bullets some of which were attempting to remove themselves from the scene and posed no obvious threat. Collins notes that individuals and groups experiencing the hot emotional rush of a forward panic undergo a changed state: "we did not feel anything ... we were past feeling anything for ourselves", said one soldier recounting his experience of Vietnam and concomitant devastation of a village and its people (Collins, 2008, p. 87). During forward panics, individuals and groups experience an altered state of consciousness born of an alien self where (in this case), soldiers "go into the emotional tunnel of violent attack, then back out of it at the end … in the aftermath they treat their own behaviour as if it were a separate reality" (Collins, 2008, pp. 87–8). A further aspect of forward panic of particular salience invoking the broader situational context for Nisour Square, is the nature of the guerrilla war in both Iraq and Afghanistan where there is a "hidden enemy and strong suspicions that the normal surrounding and civilian population are a cover for sudden attacks" (Collins, 2008, p. 88). As Mark Hulkower, Slough's defence lawyer argued "security contractors in Iraq work in 'an extraordinarily challenging environment', where the enemy does not wear uniforms, unless disguised as Iraqi soldiers or police to exploit civilians" (Thompson, 2008).

Clearly then, attempts to explain the Nisour Square killings need to be cognisant of a pathway of factors crystallising in a particular place and at a specific moment. Whether or not Slough's father drank too much is by and large inconsequential. Rather, the interactional chain giving rise to this particular incident is comprised of a complex of situational and other factors, including, it is argued here, the expectations of the Blackwater PSD and their professional culture. Previous incidents of a similar kind – although of a different scale – point to Blackwater's culture of licence where over-response may have become ingrained practice in the security practices of these men,[14] particularly given the anomalous legal status of the PMSC industry in Iraq at the time. However, while the explanatory model of the forward panic affords an enhanced sensitivity to the situational factors leading to violence, the most striking aspect of military or militarised violence as

---

[14] I would like to thank Professor Tony King for drawing this to my attention.

indicated, is that it often involves extreme brutality as noted here in the illustrative example of domestic violence where:

> Soldiers terrorise their partners in unique ways reminding the women of the bare handed skills they acquire in training ... [they] are more likely to use weapons ... [and] strangle their wives until unconscious.
>
> (Ellison & Lutz, 2003, p. 2)

This observation invites further consideration of Collins' forward panic framework where, hitherto soldiers' and veterans' bodies have remained absently present. While it is acknowledged that forward panic is not simply a physiological process, as it is also shaped by adrenalin-arousal factors leading to unpredictable actions (Collins 2008, p. 92), a focus on the embodied realm of situational practice can illuminate the specific impact of the military or militarised body. The question of proficiency in violence is highly salient in the case of soldiers who – as they roar down the tunnel of forward panic – take with them bodies trained to kill and injure others. If it is indeed the changed state of the alien other engendered through the situational contingencies of the tunnel that provide for the pre-reflective unleashing of violence, then how are we to understand the processes by which this disposition is lodged deep in the soldierly body? What is it about soldierly bodies that seem to provide for extreme levels of violence?

Colonising the Pre-Reflective: Crafting Bodies for Violence
As Ken Plummer notes:

> Lived life is a dialectical compound of self and society and the organic matrix of body and mind ... we must acknowledge that experiencing individuals can never be isolated from their functioning bodies and their constraining social worlds –

there is no room for a bodiless idealism or a mindless materialism. Body, mind, context, society – *all* are in constant engagement with each other and *all* need to be taken into account.

(Plummer, 1983, p. 54; *original emphasis*)

Phenomenological perspectives see the body and mind as seamless entities, where the body is understood as the medium by which everyday social life is realised through the practical consciousness nested in the pre-reflective realm (Giddens, 1984; Crossley, 1995; Katz, 2002; Coole, 2005; Hockey, 2009). Bodies can be said to have a life of their own with their sentience going beyond the component elements of the blood, flesh, tissue, bone and skin of which they are comprised. Invoking the theoretical understanding of Merleau-Ponty, Crossley argues that:

Our principle relation to our world is not a matter of "I think" … but rather "I can" … the "I" is misleading in this phrase because it suggests … the reflective and reflexive subject … but the "can" clearly conveys … understanding that our primary relation to our environment consists in *practical competence*.

(Crossley, 1995, p. 53 *emphasis added*)

The things we label body and mind are more appropriately conceived of as undifferentiated entities, cultural phenomena that are two sides of the same coin (Csordas, 1993, p. 140; Hockey, 2002). Given my argument that pre-reflective aspects of embodied trajectory can rise to the surface in the tunnel of forward panic, what can be said of Slough's skill sets put to such devastating use in Nisour Square? As a further strand of his defence intended to underscore military professionalism, he writes:

112

I joined the United Sates Army in August 1999 and received extensive training in both rifles and machineguns. I have successfully completed all qualification courses required by the U.S.Department of State to carry the M4 rifle, Glock 9mm pistol, M3203 grenade launcher, M249 machinegun, M240 Machinegun, Remington 870 shotgun, and have had familiaization instructions on the AK47.

If we are to believe that the Blackwater contractors sensed that contact had been initiated at Nisour Square, whether through small arms fire or a distant explosion, the PSD probably experienced a "stress, intensity and speed [of their own movements] ... via a vast surge of collective energy" (Hockey, 2009, p. 482) and, in turn, rapidly carried out collective weapon drill. This drill represents a key aspect of their collective somatic mode of attention, an embodied state of readiness applicable across social practice more widely,[15] but with particular salience to military and former combat trained individuals who have distinct ways in which they objectify their bodies in relation to one another (Csordas, 1993, p. 138). As Hockey notes in his embodied sensitivity to infantryman training in the British Army, training drills:

> Consist of programmed repetitive actions, designed to effect particular bodily practices ... there are drills for ... weapons handling ... [and] for the use of the bayonet on the enemy.
>
> (Hockey, 2002, p. 156)

It will be recalled that Slough's reference to corporeal transformation foregrounded haptic expertise in relation to a wide range of weaponry. Ultimately, these abilities penetrate

---

[15] Crossing a busy road requires that (civilian) pedestrians routinely adopt a specific somatic mode of attention designed to mitigate the very real threat of injury and even death.

the very being of those involved through the pre-reflective realm by remaking the mind-body nexus. Though these pre-reflective embodied skill capitals may lie at the heart of combat effectiveness, the extremes of violence liberated in the tunnel of forward panic can lead to uncontained levels of spill-over violence in the case of soldiers and veterans, a concern now taken up in relation to questions of responsibility and habituated social practice.

Discussion: Military Embodied Responsibility
Human agents' openness to habituated practice comes into sharpest focus for those who have been immersed into the embodied regimes of military life where the most intense and protracted of corporeal regimes can be found. As Shilling puts it in a general sense:

> Habits seep into the furthest recesses of the body. They have a structural basis in the nervous system, shape the selections our senses make, condition our preferences, predate and provide a basis for our deliberative orientations to the environment, direct our muscular responses, and structure our identities.
>
> (Shilling, 2008, p. 13)

Delving deeper into the force of habit to which we routinely refer, it is argued in phenomenological terms that "in habitual life – in bodily intentionality – it is *not* the case that I *first* get the 'thing' and *then* pass an interpretive judgement; rather, it is only *as* already interpreted" (Russon, 2004 p. 299; emphasis in original). Etched deep into the somatic memory, embodied habits can lie dormant in the individual for decades. As Campbell notes in regard to habit, "every single deliberate, freely-chosen [or coerced] ... action contains the potential to become the first step in the construction of an unconsidered and

114

automatic, habitual routine of conduct" (Campbell 1996, p. 163). In respect of British army infantrymen, Hockey notes that:

> Fighting practices are learnt ... and the practical intelligence they instil in the body comes sharply into play in extreme situations ... it is this practical intelligence which allows the infantryman to ... destroy others.
>
> (Hockey, 2002, p. 158)

Given the centrality of habit to social practice then, it is argued that what is needed is a phenomenology of responsibility (Russon, 1994, p. 298) that avoids the binary framing of unrealistic voluntarism on the one hand and paralysing fatalism on the other (Coole, 2005, p. 125). Untimely, brutal and exceptional deaths demand perpetrators be held to account for their actions. And, responsibility for the use of weapons and bare hands against unarmed, weaker others is surely to be found in the intent of individuals and groups that perpetrate such atrocities. Criminal justice systems of relevance to the current discussion depend on an individual perpetrator, Slough, who can be found to have responsibility. The wellspring of this responsibility is typically considered to be the mind, within the context of rational actors constructed through notions of premeditation, mental function, deliberation, intent and in respect of defence for murder, insanity and diminished responsibility.[16] This is the (male) actor "at the heart of modern

---

[16] However, whilst sensitive to the "sexual politics of Pre-Menstrual Tension" (Laws, 1983), it is worth considering that the "changed state" argued to be characteristic of PMT has at times been used in defence of those accused of murder and other criminal acts. Here a particular form of embodiment is mobilised to inflect perpetrator responsibility. See, for example: Horney (1978); Taylor and Dalton (1982); Harry and Balcer (2006).

understandings of autonomy, freedom, subjectivity and responsibility" against which the political phenomenologist Diana Coole argues (2005, p. 124). With its roots in the modernist and masculinist *episteme*, criminal justice's Cartesian mind-body dualism constitutes the actor as a voluntaristic decision maker whose ideas of agency have fused "phenomenal processes – such as consciousness, meaning-generation ... reflexivity and will" into the "unified ... figure of the ontological individual" (Coole, 2005, p. 128).

Whilst this conception of agency resonates with the subject of law in the developed polities, the model does in a limited way recognise the perpetrator's emotional state where affect is argued to influence culpability In recognising that individuals may act better than they know how (Giddens, 1984) in respect of their embodied, emotional realm – i.e. "crimes of passion" – thinking in these terms remains wedded to the rational actor model where emotion and irrationality are conflated, particularly in the case of women (Showalter, 1998). As noted above, a different approach would be to embody the actor in ways that acknowledge the body's sentience, as an unfinished project (Shilling, 1997), the capacities of which depend on pre-reflection. Taken from a phenomenological perspective, this would be to acknowledge that we both have and are bodies, and that these bodies demonstrate a proclivity towards particular social accomplishments nested in their corporal trajectories (Nettleton and Watson, 1998), in this case its military and militarised pathway. Rather than beginning with the mind as locus of rationality, our starting point would be the "perceptual, corporeal lifeworld ... where the practical intelligence of bodies condemns them to meaning" (Coole, 2005, pp. 128–9). In turn this leads me to suggest that whether or not the Blackwater veterans at Nisour Square should be punished falls outside a sociological remit, though it could be argued either way. The Blackwater PSD were responding to situational and interactional forces within the context of a well-honed proficiency in violence unleashed inappropriately and with devastating consequences through a changed state in the tunnel of forward panic. Framed in these terms, the perpetrators might not be seen as the autonomous decision-making agents constructed in law, or the wider political context where in Iraq (for example), the struggle to win hearts and minds calls for responsibility and, perhaps socially at least, deserves a perpetrator who can be held to account.

Conclusions

Informed by interactional perspectives on violence and a recognition of the embodied groundings of social life, I have argued that current explanations for the killings in Nisour Square as inhering in the good guy/bad guy dichotomy are unsatisfactory as they tend to neglect the situational and practical accomplishments of particular bodies trained in specific ways. It was also argued that military or militarised bodies' proficiency in violence can help to explain their tendency towards brutality in the tunnel of forward panic. Seen in this way, the problem turns on both responsibility and the dangers of lodging lethal skill capital in bodies. In sum, embodying violence can have far-reaching unintended effects, the likes of which are borne most heavily by military and militarised masculinities trained and mobilised in the interests – increasingly – of private power.

References

Avant, D. (2005). *The market for force*. Cambridge, United Kingdom: Cambridge University Press.

Baron, L., Strauss, M. A. & Jaffee, D. (2006). Legitimate violence, violent attitudes, and rape: A test of cultural spillover theory. *Human Sexual Aggression: Current Perspectives, 528,* 79–110.

Campbell, C. (1996). Detraditionalization, character and the limits to agency. In P. Heelas, P. Lash & P. Morris (eds), *Detraditionalization.* Oxford, United Kingdom: Blackwell.

Chatterjee, P. (n.d.). Wikileaks Iraq War logs reveal private military contractors killing with impunity. Retrieved 11 November 2010 from: http://www.alternet.org/world/ 148594/wikileaks_iraq_war_logs_reveal_private_military_co ntractors_killing_with_impunity

Collins, R. (2008). *Violence: A micro-sociological theory.* Woodstock, United Kingdom: Princeton University Press.

Coole, D. (2005). Rethinking agency: A phenomenological approach to embodiment and agentic capacities. *Political Studies, 53*(1), 125–42.

Crossley, N. (1995). Merleau-Ponty, the elusive body and carnal sociology. *Body & Society, 1*(1): 43–63.

Csordas, T. (1993). Somatic modes of attention. *Cultural Anthropology, 8*(2), 135–56.

Ellison, J. and Lutz, C. (2003). Hidden casualties: An epidemic of violence when troops return from war. National Sexuality Resource Centre Paper available at: http://nsrc.sfsu.edu/article/domestic_violence_troops_mili tary accessed 17 December 2010.

Enloe, C. (2002). Dismantling militarism, decommissioning masculinities: Demilitarization – or more of the same? Feminist questions to ask in the postwar moment. In C. Cockburn & D. Zarkov (eds), *The post war moment: Militaries, masculinities and international peacekeeping.* London, United Kingdom: Lawrence and Wishart.

Giddens, A. (1984). *The constitution of society.* Cambridge, United Kingdom: Polity Press.

Harry, B. & Balcer, C. M. (2006). Menstruation and crime: A critical review of the literature from the clinical criminology perspective. *Behavioral Sciences and the Law, 5*(3), 307–21.

Higate, P. (ed.) (2003). *Military masculinities: Identity and the state.* Westport, CT: Greenwood/Praeger.

Higate, P. (2012). "Cowboys and professionals": The politics of identity work in the private and military security company. *Millennium – Journal of International Studies, 40*(2), 321-41.

Hockey, J. (2009). "Switch on": Sensory work in the infantry. *Work, Employment and Society, 23*(3), 477–93.

Horney, J. (1978). Menstrual cycles and criminal responsibility. *Law and Human Behavior, 2*(1), 25–36.

Jeffreys, S. (2007). Double jeopardy: Women, the US military and the war in Iraq. *Women's Studies International Forum, 30*(1), 16–25

Katz, J. (2002). Start here: Social ontology and research strategy. *Theoretical Criminology, 6*(3), 255–78.

Laws, S. (1983). The sexual politics of pre-menstrual tension. *Women's Studies International Forum, 6*(1), 19–31.

Melzer, S. A. (2002). Gender, work, and intimate violence: Men's occupational violence spillover and compensatory violence. *Journal of Marriage and Family, 64*(4), 820–32.

Merleau-Ponty, M. (1962). *Phenomenology of perception.* London, United Kingdom: Routledge and Kegan Paul.

Nettleton, S. & Watson, J. (eds). (1998). *The body in everyday life.* London, United Kingdom: Routledge.

Patterson, T. (2009). Moms of slain Blackwater contractors speak on anniversary. *CNN.* Retrieved 11 November 2010 from: http://articles.cnn.com/2009-03-31/us/blackwater.falluja.anniversary_1_blackwater-jerry-zovko-falluja?_s=PM:US

Plummer, K. (1983). *Documents of life*. London, United Kingdom: George Allen and Unwin.

Rosen, L. N., Knudson, K. H. & Fancher, P. (2003). Cohesion and the culture of hypermasculinity in U.S. Army units. *Armed Forces & Society, 29*(3), 325–51.

Russon, J. (1994). Embodiment and responsibility: Merleau-Ponty and the ontology of nature. *Man and World, 27*(3), 291–308.

Scahill, J. (2007). *Blackwater: The rise of the world's most powerful mercenary army*. London, United Kingdom: Serpent's Tail.

Singer, P. W. (2008). *Corporate warriors: The rise of the privatized military industry*. New York, NY: Cornell University Press.

Showalter, E. (1998). *Hystories, hysteria, gender and culture*. London, United Kingdom: Picador.

Shilling, C. (1997). The undersocialized conception of the embodied agent in modern sociology. *Sociology, 31*(4), 737–54.

Shilling, C. (2008). *Changing bodies: Habit, crisis and creativity*. London, United Kingdom: Sage.

Smith, D. (1978). K is mentally ill: The anatomy of a factual account. *Sociology, 12*(1), 23–53.

Taylor, L. & Dalton, K. (1982). Premenstrual syndrome: A new criminal defence. *Law and Human Behavior, 2*(1), 269–87.

Thompson, G. (2008). From Texas to Iraq, and Center of Blackwater Case. *The New York Times*. Retrieved 11 November 2010 from: http://www.nytimes.com/2008/01/19/us/19slough.html

Tomsen, S. (1997). A top night: social protest, masculinity and the culture of drinking violence. *British Journal of Criminology, 37*(1), 90–102.

CHAPTER SEVEN

COMMEMORATING FATALITIES OF WAR AND NATIONAL IDENTITY IN THE TWENTY-FIRST CENTURY

Michael S. Drake

In the first decade of the twenty-first century, the war dead have become an issue across Europe. The contemporary contention of the remembrance and commemoration of the dead has been studied through a wide range of particular cases, (e.g. Verdery, 1999, Bell, 2006), but the growing destabilisation of their hitherto given meaning has not been seen as a general phenomenon for which the bodies of the war dead provide an acute and emotive focus. Beneath Europeanisation and globalisation, the bodies of the war dead form a kind of political substrate of other identifications, invested with emotive longing for community, often related in terms of sacrifice or victimisation. Such investments are made through rituals of commemoration or memorialisation in which the dead come to stand for values of contemporary society, a process that Durkheim observed analogically in his analysis of "primitive religion", *The Elementary Forms of Religious Life*, an analysis which was intended, following Rousseau's original use of the term (Rousseau, 1968, p. 84) also to apply to the modern, secular, "civil religions" of nationalism and individualism (Durkheim, 1996; Bellah, 1967).

The Dead and the Nation-State
Most notoriously, the contention of the meaning of the war dead produced riots and inter-ethnic violence in Tallinn, capital of the Baltic state of Estonia, in April 2007, when two nights of

121

rioting by elements of the ethnic Russian population of Tallinn followed the removal of a statue marking the burial site of Soviet troops from the Second World War, from its central public location to a military cemetery on the outskirts of the town. For ethnic Russian Estonians, the statue represents their sense of rightful belonging in Estonia, "a focal point for the local Russian-speaking minority's identity and self-esteem". Its removal from the centre of the city and from the site of the remains of the historic war dead therefore mirrors the sense of social, cultural and political marginalisation of the ethnic Russian minority, around 30% of the population (Lobjakas, 2007). In neighbouring Latvia, remembrance of the Second World War dead is tied up with resurgent anti-semitism, with proposals to prosecute Jewish partisans for war crimes against ethnic Latvians and commemoration ceremonies for the Latvian Waffen-SS involving surviving veterans, but also neo-Nazi groups.

In Germany, following a long period in which the German experience of the Second World War remained overshadowed and muted first by self-repressive silence and then after the 1960s by guilt over the Holocaust, the ambivalence of German suffering in the Second World War, particularly the effects of mass Allied bombing which targeted entire cities, was evoked by W. G. Sebald (2004), skilfully negotiating the politics of memory to produce an account which was sensitive to the ambiguity of German collective identity as both victims and perpetrators. This recognition of German suffering during the Second World War is, as Sebald was aware, always prone to appropriation by the extreme right, as has also been the case in Hungary in the twenty-first century, where the memorialisation of the martyrs of the 1956 Rising against Soviet domination are contested in public struggles over representation, often co-opted by the extreme right, who paste their own texts over those public monuments and in 2007 erected a large counter-monument calling for the restoration of a "Greater Hungary" directly opposite the single remaining monument to the Soviet war dead in central Budapest.

In Spain, the campaigns of the Association for the Recovery of Historical Memory since 2000 to exhume, identify and investigate the dead from the Francoist massacres during and following the end of the Civil War have met with a range of responses, from institutional resistance to demonstrations in support of the campaigns, a cause advanced by the then Socialist government's Law of Historical Memory, passed in 2006, compelling authorities to co-operate with enquiries about the redress of abuses during and after the Civil War.

Even where there is no current contention of the war dead, the memory of memorialisation has itself become politicised. Recent scholarship has often reviewed the memorialisation practices of the past to see in them a politics of memory that was hitherto invisible. British memorialisation has been subject to this process most notably in analyses of the memorials commemorating the dead of the First World War, hitherto considered uncontentious expressions of a national consensus of grief and mourning. In Ireland, the memorialisation of the civil war dead has similarly been opened to reveal its political dimensions, the ways in which the commemoration of the dead was used to construct Irish identity (Dolan, 2003).

The key text in understanding such processes sociologically is Benedict Anderson's seminal work, *Imagined Communities* (1991). In that book, Anderson avoids the pitfalls of the impasse of the debate between essentialists and constructionists about nationalism by pointing out that "the nation" is an imaginary that is nonetheless real in so far as it is shared and enacted. National identity is imagined because it is not based on face-to-face interaction, but consists of an imagined identity shared by individuals who will never meet each other. The subtlety of the book's argument is underpinned by a systematic analysis of the material, political and sociological factors which provided the conditions for the emergence and reproduction of the imaginary construct of the nation in modernity. The emotive force of this imaginary is not always benign, since nationalism was the force impelling millions into voluntary self-sacrifice in modern warfare, throwing bodies against barbed wire and bullets, as well as driving the genocides of the twentieth century.

Collective memorialisation functions as part of the process of the social construction and reproduction of the national imagined community. Commemoration is often co-opted or even inaugurated by the state, and indeed an argument can be made that this co-option of the dead is constitutive of the concept of the political state itself, as the foundations of that notion, uniting people and polity, are sometimes traced to the fifth-century BC Funeral Oration of Pericles for the Athenian war dead, reported by Thucydides in his *History of the Peloponnesian War*. Pericles' speech introduces the idea that the war dead have died for the cause of a state to which the listeners therefore owe their lives. In this formulation the dead come to represent the state as an enduring, immortal entity to which its living members are indebted, and for which they must offer their very lives. Some of the stipulations of Anderson's formulation enable us to begin to understand how it is that the war dead have become politically contentious especially now, in the early twenty-first century.

Anderson's (1991) imagined community is grounded in the idea of a bounded territory and population, dual aspects of nation-statehood that are unravelled by contemporary processes of globalisation. For a wide range of reasons, borders become more permeable and populations more mobile, resulting in the erosion of the integrity of the imagined community. Anderson is also very clear about the extent to which nationalism depended on the marginalisation and eradication of internal difference, a process which has been reversed since the later twentieth century, with the proliferation of cultural differentiations, of which multiculturalism is only a part, problematising the act of collective imagination. Another condition for the emergence of nationalism in the nineteenth and twentieth centuries was the prior development of a system of sovereign states since the Treaty of Westphalia settled the early modern European Wars of Religion. Globalisation, as is frequently observed and experienced, most particularly now, in the global attempts to manage economic crisis, structurally disempowers national sovereignty (Drake, 2010). National institutions of all kinds are increasingly unable to affect social tendencies, across economics, politics, health, agriculture, and all spheres of competence, since today the global drives the national rather than vice versa, as was the case in the later twentieth century notion of "international society". Policy formulations grounded in the notion of the national sovereign state cease to function effectively, as is the case with both neo-Keynesian and neo-monetarist economic policies in the face of global economic crisis today. Finally, the foundational character of the state in its monopoly of legitimate violence and in drawing the distinction between peace and war are undermined by new forms of warfare, both involving non-state actors and requiring states to act in concert, as they are unable to sustain the levels of investment to compete in technological developments (Hirst, 2001; Drake, 2007).

The state's capacity to manage memorialisation to co-opt the meaning of the war dead comes into question in an inverse relationship with its capacity to differentiate between peace and war and to maintain an effective monopoly of the legitimate means of violence. Erosion of those essential functions of the modern state opens up the violence of the present to question, as in the unprecedented scale of the demonstrations of 2003 against the invasion of Iraq, and in the questioning of whether the nation-state, even in its alliances with other states, is the appropriate agent to intervene, as in the challenges around UK military involvement in Afghanistan and Libya. In turn, that challenge, an outcome of the way that globalisation has eroded nation-state sovereignty, opens the question of the meaning of the war dead, both of the past and of the present.

The Invented Ritual of Wootton Bassett

In the rest of this chapter I will look at the events around the invented ritual of the commemorations at Wootton Bassett, which reflect this questioning of the meaning of the war dead but also illustrate the novel ways in which the national imaginary persists beyond the erosion of its original conditions, as fantasy, but also as brand or commodity.

From April 2007 until September 2011, the bodies of the British war dead passed through the town of Wootton Bassett en route to Oxford for the coroner's inquest that is required for these casualties because there is, in the sense of a sovereign declaration, no war, and there is no war because there is no enemy in the sense of another sovereign state whose actions could have caused these deaths. The coroner's inquest deals with the forensic dimension of the body of the war dead, reading the physicality of the body and reconstructing the material circumstances of its death and in this has proved controversial, exposing errors in military procedures and limitations of equipment which would otherwise not have received such publicity.

However, these questions arise from the context of death. The dead body in itself is empty of signification, a sign by virtue of being a human body, but because dead, stripped of the agency which presents the self and through which the body's performance generates its social meaning in life. It is imbued with meaning only through its focus for practices of memorialisation. In the USA, the commemoration of the body of the war dead is a public military-civic event, as the coffin is paraded through the hometown with military honours, but in the UK, with entirely different traditions of the military-civil relationship, there is no such equivalent. After the inquest, the body is returned to the next of kin for a private burial ceremony at which the Army *may* be present as colleagues-in-arms of the fallen. In the UK then, the social, particular meaning of the dead body is separate from its symbolic, semiotic meaning as a vessel for the investment of collective identification.

From April 2007, development work at RAF Brize Norton, the original reception point for the repatriation of the war dead into Britain, shifted the reception of the flights carrying the dead to RAF Lyneham, which meant that the coffins had to pass en route to Oxford through the town of Wootton Bassett, which had failed in its attempts to get a bypass built to carry traffic around the town.

Beginning with a simple coincidence of the passage of the hearse bearing the dead through the town on the same day as a British Legion veterans' association monthly meeting, the town developed a custom of silent observance of the passage of the bodies of the war dead, in which the townsfolk lined the sides of the road with heads bowed as the cortege passed. The only banners present were those of the local British Legion and of the Regiment to which the fallen soldier had belonged. This could be termed an "invented tradition" (Hobsbawm & Ranger, 1983). The town had not in the past shown any particular collective predisposition to honour the national dead. In fact, its own war memorial dated only from 2002, unlike those of most towns and villages in Britain where such memorials date back to the wave of monuments built to honour the dead of the First World War of 1914–18. Similarly, the town had not offered itself for this duty; the route of the bodies was entirely a temporary contingency.

A sense of local distinctiveness arose from this repeated ritual commemoration, which was threatened when press coverage produced increasing numbers of bystanders, swollen by media personnel, the wider public and by the attendance of the relatives of the deceased, whose emotional expressiveness broke the customary silence of the occasion (Jardine and Savill, 2009; BBC, 14 July 2009). Concerned to maintain the local character of the ritual, the town's civil leaders wrote and spoke publicly of the fragility of these events (Gray et al., 2009). That concern to maintain local distinctiveness also had the effect of ensuring that this recognition of the fallen did not imbue them with any particular meaning, in contrast to the ceremonial processions in the USA, which co-opted the dead into the traditional civil-military relations of sacrifice for the republic. The Wootton Bassett events remained explicitly apolitical, while still fulfilling the criteria of collective representation in honouring the fallen, a representation of UK society to itself which was in keeping with a pluralistic polity, and with a deep national ambivalence about the war itself.

Wootton Bassett effectively performed the function of contemporary collective representation in other ways, too. The town itself looked the part, especially as the cortege passed by the half-timbered Tudor-style market hall, a route lined with Georgian houses now serving as offices for small service businesses such as estate agents and florists, or as tea-rooms for the tourist trade. The national identity represented in the ritual of memorialisation of the fallen, was thus, inadvertently and coincidentally, a brand, a commodifiable concept in which

Wootton Bassett itself had a vested interest. Moreover, that identity, like the act of memorialisation which invoked it, was not simply given, but was explicitly performed. The very silence of the townspeople lining the street indicated a Britishness that was stoic and performatively undemonstrative even in its performance. Silence, here, was vocal, the declamation of a nation which neither needed nor was able to articulate itself coherently, as a cultural consensus, with one voice. Here, the multiple postmodern language games that make up contemporary public discourse found their ideal expression.

Despite the pronouncements of its civic leaders, Wootton Bassett came to quite literally "stand for" the nation. The very contingency and invention of this ritual became significant, performing the representation of a nation which was deeply invested in indebtedness and the short-term drive for capital gain that informs everyday economic life at every level from the individual liquidation of assets articulated in *Cash in the Attic* and enacted the wider lifestyle fashion for "de-cluttering", to the practices of the banking sector in creating and buying endless debt on which the economic recovery of the new millennium had depended. Here was another example of a way to make "something" (unspecified and commodifiable) out of "nothing" (the town's lack of any distinctive tradition of honouring the war dead). The affirmed localisation of the ritual of commemoration, however, enabled Wootton Bassett to represent a Britain that was frozen in the artificial space to which "tradition" has been consigned now that it no longer functions as a way of life, but becomes a performance, always ritualised and elevated above the everyday, a "special" category that belies its very claim to traditionality. This commodity character of course corresponds to a globalising world in which national distinctiveness is increasingly displaced as everyday, unreflective social practice and becomes "a culture" among other cultures, something to be performed and which consists as such only in that performance and its representation.

Conclusions

Where twentieth-century memorialisation of the war dead took the form of durable, permanent memorials and scripted rituals which co-opted the dead to the projection of national identity on to the canvas of the state, Wootton Bassett performed a digital soundbite, a modularised, commodifiable and apparently spontaneous performance of mourning isolated in time, in contrast to regular, recurrent remembrance. The memorialisation of the dead thus takes the form of collective representation of what Bauman (2000) refers to as "liquid" postindustrial society to itself, just as the durable, monumental forms of memorialisation of the war dead of the First and Second World Wars represented a "solid" industrial society. This is evidenced even in the memorialisation of memorialisation.

As a result of the mediatisation of its invented ritual, without which this recurrent event would not have been representative, but would have remained, as was probably intended, purely local in the strictest sense, Wootton Bassett itself became the subject of honorific recognition. Its media representation as standing in for Britain was initially refuted by civic leaders, who sought to keep the performance of recognition in honour of the fallen local and specific. However, just as the media circus continued to colonise the events, so other forms of popular recognition sought to honour the town that honoured the dead, such as the 15,000 motorcyclists who rode the route taken by the bodies of the dead to show their support for Wootton Bassett and by this secondary association, to themselves honour the fallen (MCN 2010). Subsequently, Wootton Bassett has been accorded the prefix of Royal, rendering its role into heritage status, an inherently marketable asset, but perhaps an appropriate recognition of the town's role as the self-representation of the contemporary nation.

References

Anderson, B. (1991). *Imagined communities: Reflections on the origin and spread of nationalism.* London, United Kingdom: Verso.

Bauman, Z. (2000). *Liquid modernity.* Cambridge, United Kingdom: Polity.

BBC, 14 July 2009, "Wootton Bassett's military tradition", at http://news.bbc.co.uk/1/hi/uk/8149081.stm, accessed 5 September 2011.

Bell, D. (ed.) (2006). *Memory, trauma and world politics: Reflections on the relationship between past and present.* Basingstoke, United Kingdom: Palgrave Macmillan.

Bellah, R. (1967). Civil religion in America. *Dædalus: Journal of the American Academy of Arts and Sciences, 96*(1), 1–21.

Dolan, A. (2003). *Commemorating the Irish Civil War: History and memory, 1923–2000.* Cambridge, United Kingdom: Cambridge University Press.

Drake, M. S. (2007). Sociology and new wars in the era of globalisation. *Sociology Compass, 1*(2), 637–50.

Drake, M. S. (2010). *Political sociology for a globalizing world.* Cambridge, United Kingdom: Polity.

Durkheim, E. (1996). *The elementary forms of religious life.* New York, NY: Simon and Schuster.

Gray, J., Bucknell, S., Baker, M., & Wannell, C. (2009). Letters: Wootton Bassett's silent tribute. *The Guardian.* Retrieved 22

February 2012 from: http://www.guardian.co.uk/uk/ 2009/jul/16/wootton-bassett-letter

Hobsbawm, E. & Ranger, T. (1983). *The Invention of tradition.* Cambridge, United Kingdom: Cambridge University Press.

Hirst, P. (2001). *War and power in the twenty-first century: The state, military conflict and the international system.* Cambridge, United Kingdom: Polity.

Jardine, C. & Savill, R. (2009, 7 July). Wootton Bassett: A very British way of mourning. *The Daily Telegraph.* Retrieved 11 December 2011 from http://www.telegraph.co.uk/ comment/personal-view/5771032/Wootton-Bassett-A-very-British-way-of-mourning.html

Lobjakas, A. (2007). *Estonia: War anniversary exacerbates ethnic divisions.* Radio Free Europe/Radio Liberty. Retrieved 10 December 2012 from http://www.rferl.org/content/ article/1076344.html

MCN (2010). *Wootton Bassett Afghan Heroes ride is a stunning success.* Retrieved 10 December 2012 from Motorcyle News: http://www.motorcyclenews.com/MCN/News/newsresul ts/General-news/2010/March/mar1510-wootton-bassett-ride-is-success

Rousseau, J-J. (1968) *The Social Contract.* London, United Kingdom: Penguin.

Sebald, W. G. (2004) (trans. A. Bell). *On the natural history of destruction.* London, United Kingdom: Penguin.

Verdery, K. (1999). *The political lives of dead bodies: Reburial and postsocialist change.* New York, NY: Columbia University Press.

CHAPTER EIGHT

GOVERNING THE BODY:
THE LEGAL, ADMINISTRATIVE AND DISCURSIVE
CONTROL OF THE PSYCHIATRIC PATIENT

Paul Taylor

Whilst much of our life-span may appear domestic in nature, occasionally our lives are punctuated with either the direct experience of, or presentation of imagery that highlights dramatic, unusual and potentially harmful activities or behaviours. In fact, our individual risk of harm is likely to be much greater than one necessarily assumes on a day-to-day basis, for example, travelling in a motor vehicle or eating a high calorie meal. Yet the rational construction of these risks is undertaken on a frequent, almost continuous basis and as individuals we develop our own frameworks of logic that make judgements over the benefits and potential harms of participating in a particular activity.

These lay judgements of risk are a naturally occurring phenomenon, but are shaped by an individual's understanding of what that particular risk may be. Lay judgements are often influenced by professional and scientific knowledge in addition to personal experience and influence from key institutions such as the media, government officials and experts. The virtues of avoiding a set of circumstances or altering behaviours that minimise potential harms are propounded and often can be observed to have legislative underpinnings (for example, public tobacco smoking restrictions in England and seat belt enforcement for motor vehicles). Enforcement strategies such as these govern a majority in society and may be intrinsic elements of agendas and discourses such as health promotion and health and safety. Such approaches to risk management have quickly become part of the cultural make-up of society, understandable of course in the context of a humanitarian concern for the health of society and public safety.

Mitigating risk is nothing new, and one particular area of risk management that has evolved has been in the area of crime control and the minimisation of harm to the public. A preventative logic has pervaded many institutions responsible for providing public protection. Of course, there have been failures and reviews of such failures have strengthened the resolve of specific institutions to think differently about their chosen approach. Criminal justice has not been alone in its attempts to mitigate the risks of criminality in society, rather psychiatry as a profession has had a key function in this process too. A medico-legal alignment has characterised an abundance of approaches to the social deviant, for example, the rise of forensic psychiatry and the physical presence of institutions designed specifically for the mentally disordered who have committed criminal offences or are deemed at risk of doing so (Mercer & Mason, 1998).

Psychiatry's function of preventing harm to others is just part of its mandate; acknowledgement must also be made that it serves to prevent harm to the person him/herself. Several scholars (see Kjellin & Nilstun, 2007 for an overview of the literature in this area) have termed this as medical paternalism, a process whereby the liberties of the individual are restricted so that medical interventions can be administered. This process takes place largely under the auspices of welfare and can frequently involve coercion and physical restrictions being placed on the body (such as hospital detention under the Mental Health Act (MHA), 1983 amended 2007). Whilst such approaches may be regarded as motivated by therapeutic concern this outlook may not be shared by those individuals who are subject to its interventions (Breeze, 1998). The justifications for limiting individual liberty therefore come under scrutiny; however, aggregated medical knowledge, coupled with official systems such as the MHA, serve to shape understandings of appropriate and inappropriate social conduct.

Libertarian, John Stuart Mill's (1859) *On Liberty* provides some illumination that for the state, or one of its agencies, to become involved in prohibiting behaviours it must maintain a cautious approach. Mill's (1859) *Harm Principle* adopts a stance whereby self-regarding actions (actions which may only impact on the individual themselves) should not be interfered with. Mill positions this statement within a framework of responsibility, suggesting that social actors can free themselves from coercion of society or the state, only through a process whereby they become responsible and accountable for their actions. The outcomes for those who are consistently sanctioned by authority structures and legislation, in the view of Mill, are potentially grave, causing a situation whereby individuals "neither obtain their fair share of happiness, nor grow up to the mental, moral, and aesthetic stature of which their nature is capable" (Mill, 1869 cited in D'Agostino, 1982: 319). For the psychiatric patient, the issue of responsibility is complex, as psychiatric knowledge has the capability to assert and suggest that individuals falling under particular diagnostic criteria may lack mental capacity, cannot make "informed decisions" or, in the judicial process, may be convicted of an offence on the grounds of "diminished responsibility".

Scholars emerging from the "anti" and "critical" psychiatry perspectives would argue that the coercive capabilities of the profession (for example, restrictions and controls over the body, mind and behaviours) take place under a veil of welfare and humanitarian concern. A discursive wrangling thus ensues with competing perspectives on the limits of legitimate state intervention to control the lives of others. Psychiatry's main opponents conceive that there is an over-use of preventative strategies. In these circumstances, the actual harm is not easily identifiable, neither is the victim (either self or others). The coercive and preventative approach that psychiatry readily uses, from a critical standpoint, does not emulate a liberal axiom of tolerance that Mill's original theorisations would support (see Levenson, 1986 for further ethical analyses of this).

Paternalism that is exercised by the state and its institutions takes place on many fronts and the author acknowledges that clinicians and practitioners undertake their work in the context of professional judgements and decision-making based on their individual and collective expertise. Furthermore, it is not the intention here to undermine the valuable work of the psychiatric profession; what this chapter aims to highlight is the significance of psychiatry's role in social control and participation in defining discourses and the meaning of risk.

The Politics of Risk and Risk Management
The way in which risk is imagined is fluid and dynamic and there is a prevailing cultural preoccupation with its management in what has been coined broadly as the "risk society" (Beck, 1992; Giddens, 1999). Insurances against risk are commonplace and take a variety of forms, for example, the welfare state (Giddens, 1999). Particular to crime control, risk has become institutionalised and individuals who pose the most risk to the majority have increasingly been defined as "the dangerous". The injurious effects of this have potential to be enduring; yet assumptions are typically based upon subjective judgements. McGuire (2004 cited in Hewitt, 2008, p. 187) raises concern that "socially constructed facts and conceptual

136

uncertainties, which inform public perception of risk, may correspond only loosely to the threats posed in reality". The presence of risk requires individuals and society's institutions to risk manage their actions and therefore a risk aversion mentality becomes enshrined in the legislative/policy structure that governs society.

Control of situations or individuals that threaten the social milieu is undertaken systematically and, as Lyon (2001) suggests, by virtue, a risk society is a surveillance society. Crime and danger are central to how risk may be conceived or understood; however it is only with a knowledge of the extent of crime, for example, that the true extent of the risk can be contemplated. Fear of crime is influential in the shaping of policy, legislation and public opinion on this subject, indeed, Jupp, Davies & Francis (2003, p. 144) suggest that "there was no fear of crime in Britain until it was discovered in 1982" following innovations in publicly accessible crime surveys. Through these processes of attention and social and political reaction, particular types of offender, for example, the sex offender, violent offender and the mentally disordered offender occupy a particular position in the social psyche in which they are typified in a hierarchy of those who have a propensity to cause the most devastating and long-lasting harm or injury. The measures put in place to insure against these potential threats, and the news reporting of them shape their construction and identity and they become a "major source of fear and anxiety" (Greer, 2003, p. 1).

Preoccupation with the avoidance of harm therefore becomes impressed upon the lives of all citizens and the risk estimations serve to make the "future become ever more absorbing, but at the same time opaque" (Giddens, 1999, p. 4). For the state, surveillance and control hold the key to circumnavigating social threats, however, as Rose (1998, p. 179) notes, "the task for psychiatric professionals is now less therapeutic than administrative: administering problematic persons on a complex terrain in an attempt to control their future conduct".

Systems of monitoring and control of the psychiatric patient in the less restrictive context of the community have had a problematic history. As a result of the removal of the physical or material systems of control (for example the hospital building) in favour of pharmaceutical control and visitations (for example, depot injections and community-based practitioners), psychiatrists and politicians have had the uncomfortable experience of apologising to society when things have gone wrong. The rhetoric association of dangerousness, risk and mental disorder has advanced at a significant pace, not least during the early 1990s. The murder of Jonathan Zito at a tube station in London in December 1992 by Christopher Clunis sparked fury and opened the debate on the abilities of health and allied services to manage those diagnosed with mental disorder in the community. This tragedy was marked by systematic failures in the continuity and supervision of Clunis, who had contact with over thirty psychiatrists and ten inpatient episodes for the assessment and treatment of a psychotic illness prior to Zito's murder (Coid, 1994). A report into the circumstances surrounding these events concluded that opportunities had been missed by health professionals (Ritchie, Dick & Lingham, 1994) and called for revised and robust measures for supervision in the community.

Parliamentary responses to the perceived crisis of dangerousness in society amounted to a rapid addition to the MHA (1983). Section 25a MHA (1983) "Supervised Discharge" was introduced under the Mental Health Act (Patients in the Community) (1995) in a move to counteract Health Secretary Frank Dobson's concerns that "too many vulnerable patients were being left to cope on their own, creating a danger to themselves and the public" (Dobson, 1998 cited in Warden, 1998, p. 1611). The public protection agenda became centre stage with a number of calls to adopt a process of re-institutionalisation. By this time, risk and dangerousness were firmly aligned with the diagnosis of mental disorder, and catastrophic failures in supervision had a "profound effect on public confidence in mental health services" (Burns & Priebe, 1999, p. 191), overshadowing the medical advancements of this era.

Risk Mitigation and Mental Health Policy

With its origins in the nineteenth century, MHA legislation has seen several revisions, the latest being enacted in 2007. Monitoring of psychiatric treatment has been undertaken in a variety of formats for a number of centuries, such as parliamentary commissions and independent agencies. The Mental Health Act Commission was established under the MHA 1983, and recently this commission has become assimilated into a broader agency known as the Care Quality Commission (CQC). The CQC functions to evaluate how care and treatment is delivered set against governmental policies. It makes routine and unannounced inspections and engages with service users to determine the quality of care being provided.

In the context of mental health care, the CQC has already begun to synthesise findings over the recently revised MHA in 2007. The CQC report "Monitoring the use of the Mental Health Act in 2009/10" has unveiled a number of fundamental issues and concerns over the recently amended Mental Health Act (MHA). During this twelve-month review, the CQC has observed that the MHA has been used more than it ever has been before. The CQC (2010, p. 8) reports that "over the last decade, there has been a steady decline in the overall number of people treated as inpatients in mental health hospitals". Despite this however, the number of people detained under the MHA has remained at around 45,000 people per annum (in 2009/10 there were 45,755 detentions). Furthermore, the CQC (2010) draws attention towards an increase in the number of detained service users residing in low secure care environments.

These statistics apply to both National Health Service (NHS) and private sector treatment environments. Disturbingly, and in addition to the figures presented above, the CQC reports feedback from patients that "hospital life is becoming much more focused on rules and security" (CQC, 2010, p. 11) with particular reference to locked inpatient mental health wards catering for both informal and detained service users. The CQC findings also raise concern outside of the boundaries of institutional care. Caution has further been raised over the introduction of the Community Treatment Order (CTO) and this has been identified as providing opportunity for a broad use of coercive power (CQC, 2010). These findings are perhaps unsurprising for some in light of recent developments in the national field of mental health. This discipline has undergone radical shifts in policy, economic investment and legislation and is likely to see further major reforms into the second decade of the twenty-first century under developing government proposals.

Receiving Crown assent in 2007, the new MHA illustrates a considerable revisionist approach to psychiatry's compulsory powers. Capacity, autonomy and the role of compulsion in the assessment and treatment of the individual have been just some of the areas attracting critical debate. The Richardson Committee and later the Richardson Report (Department of Health, 1999a) undertook an evaluation of the reforms necessary to develop modernised mental health legislation. In its analysis, the Richardson Report (1999a, p. 6) remarked that "the Committee is convinced that the notion of capacity has an independent value and meaning the core of which is accepted by all those involved in the operation of mental health legislation". For the Richardson Committee, a focus on the individual's capacity to consent to treatment is indicative of an attention towards the best interests of the person. Further, placing capacity at the heart of legislation would, it was hoped, regulate the boundaries of compulsory admission and treatment. The government's consultation paper based on the Richardson Committee's recommendations published the following concerns over its own expert panel's comments:

> The principal concern about this approach [Richardson Report's recommendation on capacity as a central component of legislation] is that it introduces a notion of capacity, which, in practice, *may not be relevant* to the final decision on whether a patient should be made subject to a compulsory order. It is the *degree of risk* that patients with mental disorder pose, to themselves or others, that is crucial to this decision. In the presence of such risk, questions of capacity – while still relevant to the plan of care and treatment – may be largely irrelevant to the question of whether or not a compulsory order should be made.
> (Department of Health, 1999b, p. 32, emphasis added)

As Zigmond (2001) explains, such analyses of risk rather than capacity taint decisions that are made surrounding compulsion under the Act, specifically that these decisions are not necessarily medical ones; rather they are prescriptive demands on risk minimisation amounting to a "Public Protection Order". The most recent MHA has also incorporated two overarching changes; an abolition of the four categories of mental disorder in favour of a broader definition of mental disorder, and a test of "appropriate medical treatment" being introduced. It is this second aspect that has raised some concerns within academic and professional circles. The MHA 1983 made the clinician undertaking the MHA assessment responsible for evaluating whether the mental health condition was treatable. If so, and the individual was unwilling to enter hospital informally, then compulsion could be used. Within the MHA 2007, this "treatability test" has been replaced with a statement that allows for the use of compulsion under the Act conditional that there is "appropriate treatment available". Although a small alteration, this has led to concerns that compulsion may be over-used as the threshold for detention has now been substantially lowered.

Such amendments and a lowering of compulsion thresholds may have the potential to increase hospital occupancy in line with cultural understandings of what constitutes a risky individual or the fear of blame being asserted should the wrong decision be made. A case that has featured as an area of significant deliberation is that of the diagnosis of personality disorder (PD). Compulsory hospitalisation of individuals suffering with a PD, a diagnosis first included under MHA 1959, has raised some disquiet from within professional groups over the legitimacy of detention, questioning the ability of the psychiatric profession to provide adequate treatment for this particular condition (see Sarkar (2002) for an overview of the literature). Without some level of common agreement within the psychiatric profession on the ability to treat PD (and therefore whether they have capacity to consent to treatment or not) the situation remains problematic. Attention to risk, ambiguity and disagreement over treatability, and the perception of a lowered compulsion threshold have been regarded, by some, as components of a piece of legislation that is profoundly paternalistic, authoritarian and stigmatising

(Mental Health Alliance, 2007). As Prins (2008, p. 84) posits there is an "over-emphasis on the use of the law in changing behaviour" and through amendments to the MHA, many more people may be subject to its sanctions and capabilities.

Regulating Meaning: The "New" Dangerousness

Institutions in society, such as the medical profession, have been considered to have the capability to represent and regulate meaning (Cohen, 1985). Apprehension has been raised about the possible consequences of this, not least where these meanings pertain to those who may threaten the social milieu. Criminal justice and psychiatry may be observed to be implicit in this process, and theorists draw attention towards the widening of a net of control (Cohen, 1985). Examples of this concept in practice can be detected in criminal justice policy where penal populism has been seen to take an effective hold with the promotion of legislation and policy which are electorally attractive, but unfair, ineffective or at odds with a true reading of public opinion (Bottoms, 1995). Elsewhere, psychiatry has attracted similar criticism for its newly adopted broad definition of mental disorder, removal of a treatability test and introduction of Community Treatment Orders (CTOs) under the new MHA (Prins, 2008; Mental Health Alliance, 2007).

Failures in the supervision of patients and offender-patients in the community during the last decade of the twentieth century have galvanised new methodologies for the management of risk in the community. This was not something particular to psychiatry, but rather an approach mirrored by others involved under the rubric of public safety and crime control. The risk management agenda in criminal justice had adopted intolerance to liberal measures of managing offenders. The Criminal Justice Act (CJA) (2003) represented a move towards the use of a prediction and estimation becoming central to how the offender was processed by the criminal justice system. The introduction of indeterminate sentences for public protection (IPP) and the formalising of multi-agency public protection arrangements (MAPPA) under this piece of legislation embedded a cautionary principle in the management of those defined as "dangerous offenders" (s.224–236 CJA, 2003). Despite the arbitrary and multiple meanings of the term "dangerousness", its usage has become implicit in recent legislation such as s.229 of the CJA (2003):

> *s.229 The assessment of dangerousness*
> (1) This section applies where—
> (a) a person has been convicted of a specified offence, and
> (b) it falls to a court to assess under any of sections 225 to 228 whether there is a significant risk to members of the public of serious harm occasioned by the commission by him of further such offences.
>
> (Criminal Justice Act 2003)

The rhetoric of risk and dangerousness now pervades boundaries of criminal justice and mental health policy with studies such as the National Confidential Inquiry into Suicide and Homicide (Appleby, Kapur and Shaw, 2010) providing illustrations of the extent of this issue. Sixty-five convictions for homicide were recorded in 2006 perpetrated by individuals who had received psychiatric treatment in the twelve months prior to the offence (against a total of 539 homicides in the general population) (Appleby, Kapur and Shaw, 2010). Such statistical evidence raises a number of questions within professional circles as to how these figures can be reduced and what methods can be adopted to achieve it.

Statute law, empirical evidence and the developing remit of "control professions" reinforce these new sensibilities surrounding risk and dangerousness; however, new definitions present significant problems in negotiating balance between individual liberty and security. The prevailing discourses of security, protection and risk management have generated an anxiety over a number of decades. The "anti" and "critical" psychiatry movements have raised concern that such systems provide opportunities for some individuals (for example, professionals) to self-actualise whilst life chances of others (patients) are restricted (Castel, 1991). It has been widely theorised that psychiatry itself has fought to construct its own integrity at the cost of those subject to it (Foucault, 1967; Scull, 1979) whilst others have gone further to suggest that mental illness is socially constructed and used to categorise those who deviate from the dominant norms of society (Szasz, 1961).

Whilst the process of planning reforms for the MHA was being undertaken, simultaneously, revisions were being made to address further risk posed by the mentally disordered. During the late 1990s, proposals were being drawn up to accommodate what was to be defined as a new kind of "dangerous offender". These New Labour proposals were illustrative of a politics with a priority on public protection. The brutal murder of Dr Lin Russell and her six-year-old daughter Megan, and attempted murder of nine-year-old Josie by Michael Stone in July 1996 provided a significant bolstering to these new proposals. It had emerged that prior to the murders, Stone had been detained for assessment under the MHA (1983) and had been diagnosed with a personality disorder. However he was assessed as having mental capacity and subsequently released from hospital. As Rutherford (2006, p. 55) explains, "the authors of these new proposals accepted that the status quo was unacceptable". Public safety appeared to be in jeopardy from a preying risk of individuals who had slipped through the net of criminal justice and health agencies.

The Dangerous Severe Personality Disorder (DSPD) proposals of the early late 1990s were viewed as a remedy to such heinous crimes being perpetrated in the future.

Cultivating a new MHA that would support DSPD proposals was problematic and remained an area of contention, not least in the concerns of the ability to treat this condition, with some asserting that a personality disorder is very different from a mental illness because "it is essentially a developmental disorder" (Eastman, 2000 cited in Seddon, 2008, p. 29). Over the course of ten years, the DSPD programme evolved and amounted to around three hundred beds across four units (two based in prisons and two based in High Secure Hospitals) that accommodate those risk assessed and assimilated into this category. As Rutherford (2006) indicates, DSPD proposals have become illustrative of a leading example of a much wider change in criminal justice agendas.

Evaluative analysis by Tyrer et al. (2010) of the DSPD programme has been largely inconclusive in terms of establishing clear programme successes to support future economic investment in this initiative or its ethical base. This review of the programme draws attention towards the heavy financial implications associated with detaining individuals in this way and also the questionable practices where "many prisoners are moved into the DSPD programme very close to the time at which their sentence tariff is about to end" (Tyrer et al. 2010, p. 97). Scepticism over the cost effectiveness of the DSPD programme has most recently been seen in the Response to the Offender Personality Disorder Consultation (Department of Health, 2011) whereby the UK government plans to decommission the NHS DSPD units and to re-shape the services, interventions and treatments for offenders with severe personality disorder (SPD) within the prison estate.

As an example, the DSPD programme and the developed attention towards personality disorder highlight a favouring of psychiatry to remedy forms of social deviance and a degree of therapeutic optimism in how identified conditions can be addressed. However, they also illustrate the tenuous balance between security and liberty. The aura of risky populations has become the zeitgeist. As a society, and through the structural and administrative responses implemented by politics and the state, England and Wales are fearful of risk itself. Whilst the imagery of Brady and Sutcliffe were once the faces of the dangerous offender with mental disorder, these have been replaced by the facelessness of interventions and resurgence in purpose-built facilities of containment.

Control Beyond Incarceration
The CQC (2010) reports that, in a relatively short period of time, reformed legislation appears to have given way to greater use of coercive (formal treatment under the MHA) mental health treatment. Whilst a wholesale return to Victorian asylumdom (Scull, 1993; Morrall & Hazelton, 2000) may not be evident, regimes of security, actuarial discourses, incapacitation and arguably "warehousing" are pronounced and evident in modern psychiatry (O'Malley, 2004). Psychiatry has long operated its own systems of bifurcation (Cohen, 1985). Ranging from community supervision to hospitalisation, the current tendency appears to favour institutionalisation as the preferred methodology, most noticeable in an expansion in formally detained inpatients, a growth in low secure provision (CQC, 2010). In common with crime control agendas, psychiatry has become increasingly involved as a defensive agent (Hotopf et al., 2000) and implicit in the security and risk discourses that pervade society.

Whilst formal hospitalisation may be on the increase, community supervision has also received legislative attention through revisions to the MHA. Supervised Community Treatment (SCT) has been emphasised with the introduction of the CTO, a replacement of s.25a–25j (supervised discharge) of the MHA (1983). The CTO provides authority to the responsible clinician to recall a patient back to hospital subject to them being liable to be detained under s.3 of the MHA. These measures are viewed by the profession as a competent method to reduce the likelihood of deterioration in the mental well-being of an individual by minimising the risk of harm to themselves or others through swift hospitalisation (Mind, 2011).

However, much like other amendments contained in the revised MHA, the introduction of the CTO has sparked controversy. Speaking in the House of Lords debates in 2007, Conservative Shadow Minister for Health Earl Howe raised his concerns about the consequences of the CTO being enacted. Drawing from concerns already raised by the Mental Health Act Commission, Howe referred to the addition of the CTO in MHA legislation as the introduction of the "psychiatric ASBO" (Howe, 2007). Despite these frustrations and concerns with plans contained within the Mental Health Bill (2006) to validate more stringent community supervision, the CTO has maintained its position on statute and has become an increasingly used addition to psychiatry's repertoire of sanctions.

In the first full year of the revised MHA in England, 4,107 CTOs were made (CQC, 2010, p. 96). Despite this, the efficacy of the CTO has come under scrutiny in a review of their usage internationally. A Cochrane Review of CTOs established that where used, compulsory community treatment offered "no significant difference in health service use, social functioning or quality of life compared with standard care" (Kisely, Campbell and Preston, 2011, p. 2). Whilst the efficacy of the CTO is being challenged, the CQC has also explored how they are used. In a review of 208 reports analysed by the CQC (2010) three alarming themes emerged. Firstly, one third of the sample was receiving medication for their mental health condition above the advisory limits of the British National Formulary. Secondly, whilst the CQC note the difficulties of obtaining accurate statistical data in this area, they report that in the sample analysed, there was evidence of a disproportionate use of the CTO amongst black and ethnic minority groups. Lastly, the CQC report that one third of their sample placed on a CTO has no reported history of non-compliance or disengagement with treatment.

Given the data presented by the CQC, the legitimacy of the use of the CTO is questionable. The veil of risk prevention, actuarial practices and surveillance has emerged from the radical revisionist approach to mental health law. Psychiatry has re-established and intensified its position as a key agent in the control and regulation of the meaning of risk and dangerousness. Failures in supervision of the past haunt policies of the present where "the reality is that community care is a makeshift policy of competing pressures for control" (McCann, 1998, p. 60). Whilst such policies and interventions may address human suffering and limit the potential for harm, as is evident from this CQC report, it is only now that some indication is available of the broad approaches and coercive powers of a discipline that is professionally somewhat distanced from the criminal justice system, yet has an equal ability to apply an array of sanctions legitimised through its self-regulating authority over the right to treat the treatable and attempt to treat the untreatable.

Conclusions

The revisions to the MHA and associated policy and programme developments in the field of psychiatry have developed a situation of a systematic growth in diagnosis and detention. Social deviance is increasingly becoming medicalised and psychiatry is required to engage with a broader mandate. Medical paternalism has a firm hold and assessment and treatment are not solely located within the ambition to treat; rather psychiatry must adhere to broader approaches to the social deviant and prevailing discourses of risk management and physical controls. The modern psychiatric treatment environment has therefore become part of a broad "expurgatory system" (Mathiesen, 2006, p. 141) designed to provide accommodation and arrangements for those in society who are problematised or diagnosed. Diagnosis is therefore a tool, and as such any person who is diagnosed is subject to further assessment in terms of risk discourses, and in some cases may identify them as unmanageable. In such cases further systems to ensure public safety are imposed in a bid to provide insurances against potential breaches of wider society's security (Corbett and Westwood, 2005).

The encompassing framework of psychiatry, diagnosis and the removal of a treatability test in the new MHA provide, in the view of some, a panacea for the regulation of society. They are symbolic of new strategies for crime control and social obedience. Arguably psychiatry has become an agent or tool of crime control, more so than being strictly a rehabilitative endeavour. Risk has become institutionalised within governing agencies and disciplines but has also been internalised by society's citizens. The MHA (2007) and CJA (2003) both serve to illustrate conceptually similar objectives despite emerging from ideologically opposed worlds (therapy versus punishment). In response to the prevalence of risk discourses, governments see the need to "qualify their claim to be the primary and effective provider of security and crime control" (Garland, 1996, p. 449). Such an achievement is problematised by high profile failures and harm perpetrated by a minority. However, a predicament emerges, where new categorisations and new aggregated identities of the dangerous shape the sensibilities of policies to control them and the general public who are supposedly protected by the sanctions imposed.

References

Appleby, L., Kapur, N. & Shaw, J. (2010). *National confidential inquiry into suicide and homicide by people with mental illness: Annual Report – England and Wales 2010*, University of Manchester.

Beck, U. (1992). *Risk society: Towards a new modernity*. London, United Kingdom: Sage.

Bottoms, A. (1995). The philosophy and politics of punishment and sentencing, in C. Clarkson and R. Morgan (eds), *The politics of sentencing reform.* (pp. 17–50). Oxford, United Kingdom: Clarendon Press.

Breeze, J. (1998) Can paternalism be justified in mental health care? *Journal of Advanced Nursing, 28*(2), 260–65.

Burns, T. & Priebe, S. (1999). Mental health care failure in England: Myth and reality, *British Journal of Psychiatry, 174,* 191–2.

Care Quality Commission (2010). *Monitoring the use of the Mental Health Act in 2009/10.* London, United Kingdom: Care Quality Commission.

Castel, R. (1991). From dangerousness to risk. In G. Burchell, C. Gordon & P. Miller. (eds), *The Foucault effect: Studies in governmentality* (pp. 281–98). Hemel Hempstead, United Kingdom: Harvester Wheatsheaf.

Cohen, S. (1985). *Visions of social control.* Cambridge, United Kingdom: Polity Press.

Coid, J. W. (1994). The Christopher Clunis Inquiry. *The Psychiatrist, 18,* 449–52.

Corbett, K. & Westwood, T. (2005). Dangerous and severe personality disorder: A psychiatric manifestation of the risk society. *Critical Public Health, 15*(2), 121–33.

Criminal Justice Act (2003). Retrieved 2 June 2011, from: http://www.legislation.gov.uk/ukpga/2003/44/contents

D'Agostino, F. (1982). Mill, paternalism and psychiatry. *Australasian Journal of Philosophy, 60*(4), 319–30.

Department of Health (1999a). *Report of the Expert Committee: Review of the Mental Health Act 1983.* London, United Kingdom: Her Majesty's Stationery Office.

Department of Health (1999b). *Reform of the Mental Health Act 1983: Proposals for consultation.* London, United Kingdom: Her Majesty's Stationery Office.

Department of Health and National Offender Management Service (2011). *Response to Offender Personality Disorder Consultation.* London, United Kingdom: Her Majesty's Stationery Office.

Foucault, M. (1967). *Madness and civilization: A history of insanity in the Age of Reason.* London, United Kingdom: Routledge.

Garland, D. (1996). The limits of the sovereign state: Strategies of crime control in contemporary society. *The British Journal of Criminology, 36*(4), 445–71.

Giddens, A. (1999). Risk and responsibility. *Modern Law Review, 62*(1), 1–10.

Greer, C. (2003). *Sex Crime and the Media.* Cullompton, United Kingdom: Willan.

Hewitt, J. L. (2008). Dangerousness and mental health legislation, *Journal of Psychiatric and Mental Health Nursing,* 15(3), 186–94.

Hotopf, M., Wall, S., Buchanan, A., Wessely, S. & Churchill, R. (2000). Changing patterns in the use of the Mental Health Act in England 1984–1996. *British Journal of Psychiatry, 176*(5), 479–84.

Howe, F. (2007). Mental Health Bill (HL), House of Lords Debates. 26 Feb 2007, Column 1418.

Jupp, V., Davies, P. & Francis, P. (2003). *Doing criminological research.* London, United Kingdom: Sage.

Kisely, S. R., Campbell, L. A. & Preston, N. J. (2011). Compulsory community and involuntary outpatient treatment for people with severe mental disorders. *Cochrane Database of Systematic Reviews,* 2. Art. No.: CD004408.

Kjellin, L. & Nilstun, T. (2007). Medical and social paternalism. Regulation of and attitudes towards compulsory psychiatric care. *Acta Psychiatrica Scandinavica, 88*(6), 415–9.

Levenson, J. L. (1986). Psychiatric commitment and involuntary hospitalisation: an ethical perspective. *Psychiatric Quarterly,* 58(2), 106–112.

Lyon, D. (2001). *Surveillance society: Monitoring everyday life.* Maidenhead, United Kingdom: Open University Press.

Mathiesen, T. (2006). *Prisons on trial.* Winchester, United Kingdom: Waterside Press.

McCann, G. (1998). Control in the community. In T. Mason and D. Mercer (eds), *Critical perspectives in forensic care.* Basingstoke, United Kingdom: Macmillan Press.

Mental Health Act (1959). Retrieved 2 June, 2011 from: http:// www.legislation.gov.uk/ukpga/Eliz2/7-8/72

Mental Health Act (1983). Retrieved 2 June 2011 from: http://www.legislation.gov.uk/ukpga/1983/20/contents

Mental Health Act (2007). Retrieved 2 June 2011, from: http://www.opsi.gov.uk/acts/acts2007/ukpga_20070012_en_1

Mental Health Alliance (2007). *The Mental Health Act 2007: the final report.* Retrieved 2 June 2011 from: http://www.mentalhealthalliance.org.uk/news/prfinalreport.html

Mental Health Bill (2006). Retrieved 2 June 2011, from: http://webarchive.nationalarchives.gov.uk/+/www.dh.gov.uk/en/Publicationsandstatistics/DH_063423

Mercer, D. and Mason, T. (1998) From devilry to diagnosis: The painful birth of forensic psychiatry, in T. Mason and D. Mercer (eds) *Critical perspectives in forensic care,* (pp. 9–30). Basingstoke, United Kingdom: Macmillan Press.

Mill, J. S. (1859 reprinted 2001). *On liberty,* Ontario, Canada: Batoche Books.

Mind (2011). *Briefing 2: Supervised community treatment.* Retrieved 6 June 2011, from: http://www.mind.org.uk/help/rights_and_legislation/briefing_2_supervised_community_treatment

Morrall, P. & Hazelton, M. (2000). Architecture signifying social control: The restoration of asylumdom in mental health care? *Australian and New Zealand Journal of Mental Health Nursing, 9,* 89–96.

O'Malley, P. (2004). *Risk, uncertainty and government.* London, United Kingdom: Glasshouse Press.

Prins, H. (2008). The Mental Health Act 2007 (a hard act to follow). *The Howard Journal of Criminal Justice, 47*(1), 81–5.

Ritchie, J. H., Dick, D. and Lingham. R. (1994). *The Report of the Inquiry into the Care and Treatment of Christopher Clunis.* London, United Kingdom: Her Majesty's Stationery Office.

Rose, N. (1998). Governing risky individuals: The role of psychiatry in new regimes of control. *Psychiatry, Psychology and Law, 5*(2), 177–95.

Rutherford, A. (2006). Dangerous people: Beginnings of a New Labour proposal. In T. Newburn & P. Rock (eds), *The politics of crime control: Essays in honour of David Downes* (pp. 51–90). Oxford, United Kingdom: Oxford University Press.

Sarkar, S. (2002). A British psychiatrist objects to the Dangerous and Severe Personality Disorder proposals. *The Journal of the American Academy of Psychiatry and the Law, 30,* 6–9.

Scull, A. (1979). *Museums of madness: The social organization of insanity in nineteenth century England.* London, United Kingdom: Allen Lane.

Scull, A. (1993). Museums of madness revisited. *Social History of Medicine, 6*(1), 3–23.

Seddon, T. (2008). Risk, dangerousness and the DSPD Units. *Prison Service Journal, 177,* 27–31.

Szasz, T. (1961). *The myth of mental illness.* New York, NY: Harper & Row.

Tyrer, P., Duggan, C., Cooper, S., Crawford, M., Seivewright, H., Rutter, D., Maden, T., Byford, S. & Barrett, B. (2010). The successes and failures of the DSPD experiment: The assessment and management of severe personality disorder. *Medicine, Science and the Law, 50,* 95–9.

Warden, J. (1998). England abandons Care in the Community for the mentally ill. *British Medical Journal, 317* (7173), 1611.

Zigmond, A. S. (2001). Opinion and debate: Reform of the Mental Health Act 1983: the Green Paper. *The Psychiatrist, 25,* 126–8.

Index

Index

Index

United States of America (USA), 127, 128,
using women, 6, 30–35, 37, 38, 40–42

victim, 24, 39, 100, 103, 109, 121, 122, 136
violence, 19, 39, 99–100, 104–119, 121, 125

war, 4, 5, 8, 121, 122–124, 129–130
war dead, 4, 121–130
weight-loss (see also, obesity), 5, 12, 17–18, 21–22, 25
welfare, 16, 17, 134, 135, 136
Wengraf, T., 57
Wootton Bassett, 126–127, 128, 129, 130

Young, J., 55

zombie body, 5, 18–23, 24